Freelancing Made Simple

Larry E. Hand

Margaret Heinrich Hand, Contributing Editor

Edited and prepared for publication by New England Publishing Associates, Inc.

A Made Simple Book

DOUBLEDAY   New York London Toronto Sydney Auckland

Edited and prepared for
publication by New England Publishing Associates, Inc.
Copy Editor: Joanne Wlodarczyk
Page Composition: Christopher X. Gagnon, Desktop Solutions, Inc.
Administration: Susan Brainard Matterazzo

A MADE SIMPLE BOOK
PUBLISHED BY DOUBLEDAY
a division of Bantam Doubleday Dell Publishing Group, Inc.
1540 Broadway, New York, New York 10036

MADE SIMPLE and DOUBLEDAY are trademarks of Doubleday,
a division of Bantam Doubleday Dell Publishing Group, Inc.

Library of Congress Cataloging-in-Publication Data
Hand, Larry E.
    Freelancing made simple / Larry E. Hand : edited and prepared for
    publication by New England Publishing Associates. Inc.
    p.   cm.
    "A Made Simple Book"
    Includes bibliographical references and index.
    1. Self-employed.   2. Home-based businesses   3. Service
    industries—Management. 4. New business enterprises—Management
    I. New England Publishing Associates.   II. Title.
    HD8036.H36 1995
    658' .041–dc20   94–24983   CIP
    ISBN 0-385-47466-0

ACKNOWLEDGMENTS

Special thanks go to Mickey, Joan, and Beth; Earl and Zera Hand; Elizabeth and Ed Knappman; George Baker; Rosie; Spike; Casey; Casper; Dee Dee; Mitzi; and Roscoe.

CONTENTS

Preface **About This Book** *11*

PART ONE: **WHAT IS FREELANCING?**

Chapter 1: **An Overview of Freelancing:**
A Way of Life...And No Commuting *15*
It's Not for Everyone *16*
A Matter of Priorities *17*
Planning Is Essential *17*
How It Looks on Paper *18*
Personally Speaking *18*
Money Really Does Matter *19*
Potential for Savings *20*
Family Affairs Are Key Elements in Freelancing *21*
A Plan of Attack Is Necessary *21*

Chapter 2: **Getting Down to Particulars:**
Common Freelancing Occupations *23*
Working with Computers *24*
Special Skills *24*
New and Emerging Fields *25*
A Closer Look *25*
Advertising and Public Relations Agent *25*
Bookkeeper *26*
Computer Consultant *27*
Craft Artisan *27*
Desktop Publishing *28*
Elderly Assistance Service Operator *29*
Furniture Restorer/Refinisher *30*
Videographer *31*
Woodworker *32*
Writing and Editorial Services *33*

PART TWO: WHO ARE FREELANCERS?

Chapter 3:   **On the Fence But Ready to Jump:**
Are You a Freelancer?   *37*
Chief Qualities of Freelancers   *38*
Confident, Yet...   *40*
Ability to Size Yourself Up   *41*

Chapter 4:   **It's a Lonely World, But You're Not Alone**
You're One in a Million...Five Million...Twelve Million...   *46*
Freelancing Isn't Gender Specific   *48*
Working Alone, But Staying Connected   *49*
Connecting the Modern Way: E-Mail and Life on the
"Highway"   *51*

PART THREE: WHEN IS IT TIME TO FREELANCE?

Chapter 5:   **The Time to Go for It**
Dreams Have a Way of Turning into Reality   *55*
When the Market Will Bear It   *57*
Going from Part-Time to Full-Time   *59*
Consider the Seasonal Aspects   *59*
One Last Test to See if You're Prepared   *60*

Chapter 6:   **Deadlines and Dilemmas:**
Managing the Business Schedule   *61*
Develop a Project Plan   *62*
A Plan to Manage the Plans   *64*
Establishing Priorities   *65*
Tracking and Analyzing Your Business Time   *66*

PART FOUR: WHERE DO YOU FREELANCE?

Chapter 7:   **Teenage Daughters Don't Always Understand**
Maintaining a Balance in Your Business and Personal
Lives   *72*
The Basics of Balancing   *73*
At Home, Advantages and Disadvantages Are Often the
Same   *75*
Family, Friends, and Business   *76*
Defining Your Work Space   *79*

Chapter 8: **The Freelancer's Workplace**
Take Inventory and Make a Wish List   *82*
How to Buy a Computer System   *84*
Don't Forget the Peripherals   *87*
Choose Software That Fits Your Needs   *88*
Now, Gather Up Your Belongings...   *88*
Customizing the Work Space   *89*
Keep Up with the Times   *90*

PART FIVE: **HOW DO YOU FREELANCE?**

Chapter 9: **Legalities and Technicalities**
When in Doubt, Seek Help   *94*
Assuming the Right Form of Business for You   *95*
Sole Proprietorship   *95*
Partnership   *95*
Corporation   *96*
Getting Down to Business   *97*
Zoning and Home-Based Businesses   *98*
Making Sure Independent Means Independent   *100*
Putting It in Writing   *102*
Protecting Your Assets   *102*
Don't Let the Tax Man Get You   *103*

Chapter 10: **Money and Motives**
The Profit Motive   *106*
Establishing a Pricing Schedule   *106*
Looks Are Deceiving   *107*
Assess Where You Fit into the Market   *109*
Your Money or Theirs?   *111*
Budget Isn't a Dirty Word   *111*
Home-Based Considerations   *112*
Keeping Expenses in Line   *113*
Freelancing and Personal Debt   *114*
Record Keeping and Computer Software   *114*
Managing the Cash Flow   *115*

Chapter 11: **Yes, You Have to Sell—And Keep Selling**
In the Beginning...   *120*
Marketing a Service   *120*
The Never-ending Story—Finding and Keeping Customers   *122*

Mounting Your Campaign   *123*
Advertising   *123*
Public Relations   *124*
A Final Word on Communicating: Everybody Needs a
Copy Editor   *125*

Chapter 12: **A Matter of Degrees**
From Hobby to Profession   *128*
If You Just Want to Moonlight   *131*
From Part-Time to Full-Time   *131*
Cutting the Ties: From Employed to Self-employed   *132*
Financing   *132*
Image   *133*
Expanding an Existing Freelancing Business   *133*

Chapter 13: **A Road Map:**
How Do You Get There from Here?   *137*
First, the Mistakes...   *138*
Then, Some Preventive Medicine   *138*
Get a Plan   *139*
The Business: Its Scope and Purpose   *139*
The Market: Its Size and Characteristics   *140*
Equipment and Physical Requirements   *140*
Management and Staffing   *141*
Financial Requirements and Projections   *141*
Working Within the Plan to Meet Day-to-Day
Requirements   *141*
Cash Flow Tips   *141*
Tax-Savings Tips   *142*
Don't Nickel-and-Dime Yourself into Bankruptcy   *143*
Get Money Up Front   *144*
Insurance and the Freelancer   *144*
Retirement Planning   *146*
Never Stop Listening   *148*
Set Up a Record-keeping System You Will Use   *149*

PART SIX: **WHY DO YOU FREELANCE?**

Chapter 14: **Motivating Factors**
...left a good job in the city...   *154*
Yes, Do Try This at Home   *155*

Where the Jobs Are Expected to Be   *155*
Rely on More Than Statistics   *157*

APPENDIX

Associations and Organizations
General Associations and Organizations   *159*
Specialty Associations and Organizations   *162*
Computer Services   *166*
Directories   *167*
Financing Information and Financing Sources   *167*
Government Agencies   *169*
Miscellaneous Sources of Help   *174*

GLOSSARY: BUSINESS AND FREELANCING TERMS   *175*

RESOURCES: FOR FURTHER READING

Books
Advertising and Marketing   *179*
Finance   *180*
General Business   *180*
Home-Office Management   *182*
Law   *183*
Specific Occupations   *183*

Catalogs of Publishers Specializing in Small and Home-Based Business   *185*

Magazines and Other Periodicals
Published Articles   *186*

INDEX   *189*

About This Book

Freelancing. Simple. Those two words may seem to be incompatible, especially if you are one of the millions of people who have joined the ranks of the self-employed in recent years. Freelancing, definitely, is not painless. But it can be simplified and broken up into manageable pieces. You just have to figure out how to manage a lot of pieces at once. And you have to turn a profit if you're going to make a living.

This book treats freelancing just like thousands of news reporters treat a daily story—by breaking it up into bite-size pieces: What is freelancing? Who is freelancing? And when, where, how, and why are they doing it? Freelancing is not confined to such careers as writing, photography, or the arts. Within the context of this book, freelancing is any job or occupation that . . .

o A person performs as an independent contractor

o Involves working out of the home

o Derives its income from multiple clients

o Does not require professional certification or a technical license

o Mixes family, personal, and business matters

Sometimes, in today's computer lingo, freelancers are referred to as "outsourcers." In tax terms, a freelancer is an "independent contractor." Even "self-employed" is used synonymously with freelancers, although self-employed has a much broader connotation than does home-based business.

This book was written for the broad range of people who are freelancing because of one or more economic, personal, and technological factors:

o *Traditional freelancers,* who choose this life-style because of their profession and their personal aspirations.

o *Reluctant freelancers,* traditionally corporate or manufacturing employees who have been cast into the vat of self-employment as companies downsized and comparable jobs failed to materialize.

o *Women,* who are expected to own 50 percent of the country's businesses within a few years, and who are finding in many cases that their only true way to advance is through self-employment. Other women, who have young children and want to stay home with them, are inventing home-based freelance careers.

o *Retirees,* a growing and younger population segment, who have time on their hands, quite often money to invest, and many years of vitality ahead of them.

o *Handicapped people,* whose special needs can be productively met by working the right job at home. Also, parents of handicapped children can better care for them by working freelance from the home. And people who are caring for elderly parents can be freelancers.

o *Interested observers,* who toy with the idea of freelancing and, as technology such as computers and fax machines get even more affordable, are on the brink of making the plunge.

o *Seasonal freelancers,* who work or attend school during the academic year, or who play a sport during its season, then supplement their salaries working freelance the rest of the year.

These freelancers and potential freelancers are not just writers, photographers, and artists.

They are researchers, tutors, desktop publishers, professional shoppers, sitters (of pets and plants), consultants, potters, product testers, sales agents, bookkeepers, computer specialists, woodworkers, maids, pool cleaners, or home handymen and -women.

In this respect, freelancing is broad in scope and appeal and has a somewhat romantic image, which takes the edge off the harsh economic and business matters that accompany self-employment.

Whatever you call it, freelancing is a way of life and a business.

PART ONE

WHAT IS
FREELANCING?

CHAPTER ONE

An Overview of Freelancing: A Way of Life . . . And No Commuting

---

KEY TERMS

flexibility

planning

priorities

responsibility

self-reliance

self-sufficiency

The term *freelancing* conjures up as many different images in people's minds as there are occupations at which you can freelance. While you may see an opportunity to "be your own boss," another person visualizes a checkbook register and sees the lack of steady deposit entries. Or you may see an opportunity to branch out and perform a variety of tasks in your specialty area, but someone else sees the lack of support staff and visualizes taking out the garbage and filing the paperwork. Or, perhaps, you see the small jobs you take between large projects as simply a way to pay the bills. Someone else might see them as boring and mundane tasks

they'd just as soon avoid. In reality, freelancing encompasses all of these things, positive and negative.

This book emphasizes the practical, not inspirational, aspects of freelancing and offers simple explanations on the advantages *and disadvantages* of working on your own. Starting with the premise that to succeed in freelancing, you have to possess at least a little knowledge of a lot of things—or have enough money to pay someone else to worry about the details—this book deals with the traditional subjects that relate to starting and operating a business. It also deals with the concept of freelancing and how it relates to business—mainly the

OPTIONS: WHAT YOU CAN DO IN 90 MINUTES OF TIME		
Commuting by train	**Commuting by car**	**Freelancing**
Read	Drive	School Baseball Game
Balance Checkbook	Listen to Radio	Mow Lawn
Sleep		Matinee with Friend
Work on Laptop Computer		Work on Home Computer

idea that if you don't mind the business properly, you won't be a freelancer very long.

But freelancing is much more than a business: It's a way of life that also is a business. You have to weigh more than just the business factors when deciding whether, how, and when to become a freelancer, or whether to expand an existing part- or full-time freelancing business.

Probably the most appealing aspect of freelancing is being your own boss. In reality, though, that also is the most difficult aspect. Freelancing requires that you know at least a little about finance, law, zoning, bookkeeping, environmental regulations, taxes, and health insurance. Most importantly, you have to be competent, even exceptional, in your chosen profession. And as your own boss, you have to be able to decide—quite often on short notice—

what's best for you in your career. In other words, freelancing is all about **self-sufficiency.**

It's Not for Everyone

The freelancing work style suits some people. For others, spending 30–45 minutes, or an hour or more, on a train every morning and every night, five days a week, also is a way of life. They use that time to adjust their attitudes, catch up on some reading, keep up with the day's news, carry on conversations with friends or business associates, or sleep.

Freelancing from the home means no commuting time, except when you need to perform necessary on-site tasks, such as library research, sales calls, photography sessions, product deliveries, or on-site repairs. That means you have to make arrangements in your own schedule to adjust your attitude, catch up on some reading, keep up with the day's news, carry on conversations with friends or business associates, or sleep.

The table on the previous page lists some of the options that are available to commuters, while they commute, and to freelancers, who save this 90 or so minutes a day getting to and from work. While the table may not include the most productive uses for a freelancer's time, it does illustrate the **flexibility** involved in freelancing, as long as the work gets done on deadline. And in all fairness, not all car commuters drive alone. In car pools, the train options may also be available to auto passengers.

A Matter of Priorities

Freelancing constantly involves setting and resetting **priorities.** If you are employed in a regular, full-time position, your priorities are basically set for the week: You work the company's schedule at the company's location, and you tend to your family or friends whenever you can find time during the week or on the weekend. If you're freelancing—and this is assuming you have enough business lined up to plan at least a week or a month ahead—you may have the option of determining what activities take precedence on Tuesday afternoon, Wednesday night, or Thursday morning. But you also may have to work some weekend days to meet a tight schedule or to accommodate the needs of a client.

If you work late on Monday, you can be at your friend's art exhibit opening Tuesday afternoon, and you don't have to fill out a leave request. Or, since you need to meet with a client Wednesday night at the client's house, you can meet with your son's teacher Thursday morning.

Sometimes, freelancing leaves you with no choice about when you work—if you want to make the sale or get that contract that will carry you through the winter. In the freelancing world, you have to be flexible and open-minded. With one project winding down and the next not scheduled to begin within the next month, decisions have to be made on how to fill the downtime. Do you take a vacation; catch up on work around the house; visit your parents; or assuming you need the money, take that job that may mean working some extra-long hours but that will, nevertheless, pay the rent or mortgage next month?

Planning Is Essential

People with full-time jobs generally know what they are going to make in salary over the next year. In freelancing, unless you have long-term contracts that spell out pay amounts and schedules, you sometimes don't know what you're going to make next *month*. This doesn't bother some people. But others just can't live this way.

In freelancing, you have the potential to make considerably more money than you would in a salaried position—if you work harder and smarter. And since you're the boss, you can decide how to spend that money, how much of a weekly paycheck you get, and how much you put away for the future. Essentially, freelancing is a balancing act. Through careful **planning,** you try to meet your personal, business, professional, and family

ADVANTAGES AND DISADVANTAGES OF FREELANCING

Pro	Con
Personal control	Loneliness and separation
Income potential	Irregular income
Choice of work	Multitude of tasks
Family closeness	Lack of security
Professional growth	Loss of benefits
Productivity increase	Potential poor work habits
Tax savings	Tax-filing requirements
No office politics	Loss of camaraderie
No age restrictions	
Savings potential	
Solitude	

Some of these advantages and disadvantages will be covered in greater detail in other chapters of this book. But this chapter is a general overview of freelancing.

goals in the best way you know how. And it takes a great deal of **self-reliance** to make the myriad of decisions that come with the territory.

How It Looks on Paper

Freelancing can consist of a number of different jobs or occupations, some of which are detailed in the next chapter. But some common elements—advantages and disadvantages—generally apply to all freelancing businesses. The above chart shows the most common factors.

Personally Speaking

Freelancing is a personal business. You gain personal freedom, personal control, personal growth, and personal productivity. Theoretically, at least, you get to choose which jobs to take on and determine how best to complete the job. In the process, you hopefully will have gained experience and knowledge that will help you on future jobs, either in completing them faster or smarter or in setting a price that more accurately reflects your time, expenses, overhead, and profit. All of this adds up to increased personal productivity.

On the flip side, however, can be feelings of isolation and loneliness due to separation from coworkers. These feelings can lead to depression or poor personal habits, such as raiding the refrigerator too often or watching soap operas when you should be working.

If you're not the disciplined type, having so many options on how you spend your workday can lead to poor work habits. And poor work habits can go either way. You can slack off and watch too much television, take too many trips to the coffeeshop (to keep up with local news), or clean every square inch of your office just to avoid starting that project you know is going to take three long days to complete.

Then again, you can get so wrapped up in your work—just like the busy corporate executive—that you forget you promised to take your wife to lunch today, right after the allergist's appointment which you also forgot.

Perhaps you're not fond of office politics; that's one reason freelancing is attractive to you. When you're freelancing, office politics sometimes amounts to just negotiating with a daughter or friend over where to put that picture you (unfortunately) got for your birthday.

But when you leave your office and its politics behind you, you also leave behind the camaraderie of your coworkers, especially the ones who fell on your side of the political battle lines. Some people miss being able to bounce ideas off two or three other people face-to-face within minutes of thinking of those ideas.

Other people, however, need the solitude of working at home and prefer to mull over their concepts before subjecting them to others' scrutiny. There are advantages to both, and, again, it's a personal matter.

Money Really Does Matter

Depending on your skill levels—professionally and businesswise—you have the potential to earn more money in freelancing than in many comparable salaried positions, particularly when you consider the average rate of annual pay increases. But as a freelancer, your pay often comes in irregular chunks, and you have to be able to manage the cash flow.

Whereas with regular employment you can relegate the rent or mortgage to one week's salary, the car payment to the next, and the utilities to a third, you have to develop a slightly more complicated plan in freelancing. For instance, if a writer sets aside a certain block of time to research and write a magazine article, for which she receives a small advance but for which she will not get full pay for another month, the writer also has to set aside enough money from other projects to cover the bills due during that time.

The biggest financial question for freelancers is the uncertainty of income—any income at all. Consultants and advisers recommend that anyone going into business have in the bank anywhere from six months' to two years' worth of money to pay regular bills and to keep him or her going in case there is

Rev **CASH FLOW**

	WEEK 1	WEEK 2	WEEK 3	WEEK 4
ON HAND	$6,000	—	—	—
INCOME*	+2,500	0	0	0
EXPENSES	-1,200	-750	-175	-125
SALARY/DRAW	-500	-500	-500	-500
BALANCE	$6,800	$5,550	$4,875	$4,250

Assumptions: $5,000 contract with an advance of 50 percent. Income from contract broken down as follows: 45 percent going to project expenses, 40 percent to salary/draw, and 15 percent to gross profit.

a long dry spell. Loss of income could result from any number of factors, such as having a major client go out of business or having an accident that confines you to bed for a while.

A freelancer working out of the home also has to have a system for keeping personal and business finances separate. Many do this by simply paying themselves a salary if their business is incorporated or a draw if they're a proprietor or partner. Home-office expenses can be paid in various ways, depending on the form of the business, and this is treated in detail in a later chapter.

A salary or draw system helps when planning cash flow, a critical process in running a business. For instance, when a freelancer gets a 50 percent deposit or advance on a project that will take four weeks to complete, that deposit may have to be apportioned according to the entire length of the project, because the remaining 50 percent may not be received until after the work is deliv-

ered. That's where cash flow becomes important.

To calculate cash flow, a freelancer has to figure out the amounts and the due dates of all expenses anticipated during a period, then he or she has to list the amounts and the due dates of all income during the same period. A simple cash-in, cash-out chart above illustrates how expenses and a salary/draw can be apportioned over a hypothetical four-week project. From the chart we see that the final $2,500 payment (50 percent of $5,000) is necessary in order to replenish working capital (cash on hand) and yield a profit of $750 (15 percent of $5,000).

Potential for Savings

Hopefully, a freelancer can save some money by not commuting to work. There will be fewer auto and other commuting expenses and possibly less spending on office clothes and on lunches out. However, if your freelancing business requires that you meet regularly, maybe daily, with clients in your home, or if you have daily business meetings outside the home, you may not be able to save on clothing and meals.

Another savings potential comes from taxes. As a proprietor, partner, or as a corporation, you are entitled to some tax breaks that regular salaried employees do not enjoy. But the **responsibility** of filing all tax forms now lies with you and your accountant.

One area where savings probably will not be realized is health insurance. Loss of employee benefits is one of the biggest disadvantages of freelancing. But shopping around may help you spend less on insurance premiums.

Family Affairs Are Key Elements in Freelancing

Family considerations force many people to choose freelancing. If you can make a living at home, perhaps it is more important to see your children come home from school, rather than to hear them tell you by telephone about the tests they aced. Or maybe it's more important to work part-time at home during school hours, so you can be with your 6- and 7-year-olds after school, rather than working full-time and

shelling out good money to send the children to day care.

If you have a spouse who works at a salaried job, then many of the disadvantages of freelancing can be overcome, particularly if the spouse's job comes with health insurance, a retirement plan, and some long-term security. But if your spouse does not work, or if you both work at the freelancing business, perhaps the closeness of the relationship and the flexibility of your schedules is enough to compensate for the lack of financial security offered by salaried positions with paid benefits.

A Plan of Attack Is Necessary

One advantage of freelancing is you often get to pick and choose the order in which you perform some tasks, instead of working at the schedule and flow established by someone else. But the tasks that you have to perform also grow in number if you're a freelancer. Unless you're hiring a maid service, there's no automatic trash-can emptying after 5:00; you have to do it yourself, right after you sign that contract for the next $5,000 of income.

In freelancing, you may be your own chairman, or chairwoman, of the board, but you're also the janitor—and a lot of other things in between.

CHAPTER TWO

Getting Down to Particulars: Common Freelancing Occupations

KEY TERMS

competency   emerging occupations
home-based occupations   multiple clients
special skill   technology

Freelancing, by definition, is working without a long-term commitment and for more than one employer. This book concentrates on freelancing related to **home-based occupations** that, typically, require no special technical or professional certification but that do require some type of expertise.

These occupations can range from artist to zoology tutor, whatever makes money and involves work that is performed in or managed from the home for **multiple clients.** While some occupations discussed in this book may be performed by people who do have some type of technical or special certification—teachers or specialized service

providers, for instance—the emphasis is on the work itself and how it is performed on a freelance basis.

It is this area that separates freelancing from classic entrepreneurship. Most freelancers already know what they want to do, because they've developed an expertise and they may have been doing it under someone else's employ for a number of years. But a person who just wants to start a business for business's sake is an entrepreneur. Freelancing involves the same business steps as an entrepreneurship, but the goal in freelancing is to practice one's chosen profession or expertise. The goal of an entrepreneur is financial reward from *any* successful business enterprise.

Working with Computers

In today's fast-paced world, freelancing often implies working with computers in some capacity, whether it is programming, consulting, technical servicing, or simply word processing or bookkeeping. Rapid advances in **technology** have brought computers down to simpler operating environments and cheaper prices than they were just a few years ago. Families with children in school also fill retailers' aisles on weekends looking for the right machine for their children and, perhaps, one that can double as an income-producing tool.

You can buy a computer system for less than $1,000, or you can pay much more if your needs call for advanced features or considerable power. Pricing and availability of hardware and software applications has helped to open up new and expanded opportunities for freelancers working out of their homes. And an increasing number of freelancers are seizing these opportunities.

Some of the typical computer-related freelancing occupations are relatively new, but some are more traditional occupations that have been transformed by computers. Among the newer occupations is computer bulletin-board system operator. In this field, you establish a high-powered computer setup, into which subscribers can dial by modem to retrieve specialized information and software. Two fields of occupation that have been transformed by computers are editorial services and general business

services. A professional writer cannot survive economically without at least a simple computer today, and a bookkeeper is likely to post a loss on his or her own bottom line if the only business tools he or she has are a pencil and paper ledger sheets.

Computer occupations themselves change with the times. Because of the increased mobility allowed by today's high-speed modems, hand-held computers with fax capability, and ever more powerful desktop computers, computer experts are less dependent on central-office environments. A number of possibilities exist for a one-person computer business, especially one that offers hardware and software service and support to small businesses and other home-based freelancers.

But working with computers goes further than just the occupation itself for freelancers. Regardless of what you do, working effectively with a computer has a profitable effect on your business. If you have to keep track of numerous details about multiple clients, a database program speeds up the process immensely and lets you do what you do best. If you have to write a lot of letters, a word-processing program is practical and efficient. And if you do at least part of your own bookkeeping, a simple accounting program can make it easier.

Special Skills

Some freelancing occupations, however, are rooted in age-old traditions and may or may not involve using a computer. Such occupations typically depend on a person's special skills. Traditional woodworking, for instance, calls for precise craftsmanship if the freelance woodworker plans to get top dollar for his reproduction in expensive cherry wood of a 19th-century highboy. The same high level of craftsmanship is needed for, say, a potter or a quilter. And a freelance public-relations agent needs expert interpersonal skills if her client's reputation is going to improve in the community.

Every freelancer has some type of **special skill.** Otherwise, there would not be anything for him or her to market as a freelancer. These skills can range from technical to managerial to editorial to human relations to special abilities with pets and animals. The **competency** with which a person executes these skills holds the key to whether or not a freelancing business is successful.

Working as a consultant is one of the most common freelancing occupations. If you are an expert at something, then you can market that expertise directly to clients and cut out the traditional middleman: the employer.

New and Emerging Fields

There are new and **emerging occupations** that have been created because of recent technological advancements or economic trends. These occupations include writing and designing material to be distributed on CD-ROMs or running a research service that generates reports from information retrieved from computer networks. Another relatively new occupation is being a consultant to economically displaced people who want to start their own businesses because they lost their jobs when their companies downsized.

A list of the many occupations filled by freelancers is contained in the box on page 42 in Chapter 3. But a more detailed look at some freelancing occupations is presented in this chapter. While steps in the business process and some information on equipping businesses are included here, more details on these "money matters" are contained in later chapters. Also, the requirements list with each entry is intended to be a starting point only, since every freelance business is likely to have special needs and a range of financial options.

A Closer Look

Following is a closer look at some common freelancing occupations. Lists are presented to outline some of the first steps and considerations involved in getting into the field, along with some of the tangible items typically required. More specific information on start-up costs and ongoing expenses is contained in later chapters.

Advertising and Public Relations Agent

While the functions of advertising and public relations are often separate in large companies, a freelancer can be valuable to local organizations, individuals, and businesses by performing a wide range of services. A fellow freelancer who makes and sells a specialized accounting package for medical offices, for instance, cannot afford the time nor money to contract with two separate companies to get 1) a news release written and distributed and 2) a slick trade-magazine ad written, produced, and placed.

If you can do both functions, you and the other freelancer win. And if you can balance your client list with a variety of small businesses and a couple of large agencies or corporations, your advertising and public-relations freelancing can grow. Since this is a labor-intensive occupation, initial investment costs do not have to be high. You can start with basic office necessities, then add various computer capabilities and other expansions as needed.

Typical first steps and considerations

o If you're working for a regular employer now, see if there is part of your job you can take with you, emphasizing the continuity servicing an account, the savings the employer will make on benefits, and the existing familiarity with your work quality and habits.

o Scour the local, regional, and state newspapers, looking for new companies, companies that are expanding, and big companies that are downsizing. They all may need short-term advertising or public-relations help.

o Write and produce your own promotional brochure.

o Attend some local business-group meetings and talk up your venture.

o Talk to other writers, photographers, or advertising people to assess whether there are any subcontracting possibilities.

Typical requirements

o A computer system with software that enables you to write; conduct research on-line; and keep a database of clients, trends, and demographics.

o A fax machine capable of sending and receiving proofing material or a fax/modem setup to use with your computer system.

o A subscription to an on-line computer service or an Internet access provider.

Bookkeeper

Bookkeeping can be as intensive a business as you want it to be, from part-time to more than full-time. It can also be a home-based business in which you do all of your work at home or you perform a mixture of work at home and at clients' locations.

Typical first steps and considerations

o Research computer software programs available and in prominent use in your area. If you work part of the time on-site and part of the time at home, you will need to be able to transfer files back and forth, so compatibility is a key consideration.

o Identify new and expanding businesses and inquire as to their need for a bookkeeper. Many other lone freelancers would be happy to turn over this process to someone else.

o Attend tax and record-keeping seminars sponsored by state agencies and private trade organizations so that you're up-to-date on the latest legal requirements.

Typical requirements

o Besides a calculator, you'll need a computer system capable of running the software you buy (see above).

o A backup tape drive for your computer to use as extra security in case of computer or disk failure.

o Plenty of filing cabinet space for long-term storage of records.

Computer Consultant

Most people today probably think they need a computer, whether they do or not. Most businesses know they need a computer. But with the variety of computer hardware and software available on the market, people can benefit from the honest advice of a computer consultant in buying and setting up a system, then in maintaining it and upgrading it when necessary. If you've been a computer professional with a large corporation for a number of years, you just have to retool your thinking to deal with more down-to-earth clients. Experts in local area networks, hardware installation, specialty programming, and technical support can fill a definite need for small businesses that typically pay faster than larger, corporate accounts.

Typical first steps and considerations

o Take stock of your computer capabilities and specialties and create a list of services you can provide.

o Determine how many small businesses in your area might need new equipment installed, old equipment upgraded, or software programs tailored to their own needs.

o Talk to computer professionals in your existing network of associates and acquaintances to determine if there is subcontracting or referral work available.

Typical requirements

o Your own computer system with diagnostic hardware and software.

o A laptop or portable computer to use if necessary on service calls.

o Subscription to an on-line information service that allows you to search for difficult-to-obtain hardware or software.

Craft Artisan

In an increasingly impersonal world, the market for handmade crafts continues to grow, especially those that the craft artisan sells personally. Handcrafted products range from a simple ceramic spoon rest that can be used every day to an elaborate metal sculpture that has no utilitarian value except to irritate obnoxious neighbors who don't agree with the way you've decorated your side yard. Pottery is one of the most common home-based craft occupations, but blacksmithing experienced a small revival of sorts in recent years. Since this category of freelancer covers such a wide range of specialties, the following list is more general than others in this chapter.

Typical first steps and considerations

O Join a craft guild. If a local one exists, you can meet a number of other artisans in your own area who can help you get through some of the isolation you will experience as a home-based freelancer. You might also consider joining a state or national guild to get a wider perspective on your specialty and the craft business in general. You'll get newsletters from craft guilds that are both informative and advisory.

O Subscribe to and read one or more craft-related publications that apply to your specialty.

O Attend a number of art and craft shows to observe what others are producing and how their products are priced. Also pay close attention to how their booths are set up and how the artisans interact with people visiting their booths.

O If you don't want to sell your products on the craft-show circuit, visit area craft galleries and tourist shops to determine if there is a market for either wholesaling your work or selling on consignment.

O A third option is mail order. Review general-interest and specialty publications to determine what types of ads

similar artisans are running. Get ad rates and calculate what you would have to charge for your products to make a profit.

Typical requirements

O A work space that will be undisturbed by other family members or visitors, that conforms to local zoning laws, and that is big enough to accommodate growth in your business.

O At least the basic tools of your trade, plus the specialty tools that apply to your products.

O Reliable transportation for carrying your products to craft shows or for delivering them to wholesalers or consignment shops.

Desktop Publishing

Spurred by the advent of easy-to-use computers and page-makeup software, desktop publishing has blossomed into a popular cottage industry. With a relatively minimal amount of equipment, a freelancer can publish a newsletter, produce original specialty greeting cards, or make up newspaper or magazine ads. If you have a capable laser printer, you can do basically everything yourself. But many desktop publishers use their own equipment to produce items to just the proofing stage, leaving the actual printing to better-equipped printing companies.

Typical first steps and considerations

o Decide what types of products—newsletters, ads, magazines, greeting cards, etc.—you want to produce.

o Develop sources of supplies, including a computer dealer, a photography shop, a graphics supplies dealer, a service bureau for outputting items beyond your technical capabilities, and a printer.

o Determine whether there is a market for your business. One approach is to contact clubs, organizations, or businesses that can and will use a marketing tool such as a newsletter and determine whether they already have the capability to produce such a newsletter in-house or whether they would need your services. You can often get in the door by producing one product (i.e., a newsletter), then expand to other services from there.

Typical requirements

o A work area big enough and isolated enough from the rest of the house to set up the proper equipment and keep it in working order.

o A computer system, including either a Macintosh, DOS-based, or other computer with a large hard disk drive and as much random access memory (RAM) as you can comfortably afford; a large-screen color monitor (to view full pages at full-size); a laser printer; a high-speed modem; a portable storage device, such as a removable hard disk drive; and some type of backup system. (See "How to Buy a Computer System" in Chapter 8.)

o Computer software, including word-processing, illustration, charting, and page-production programs.

o A fax machine capable of sending and receiving good-quality proofs.

o A self-published brochure describing your freelancing operation.

Elderly Assistance Service Operator

In the harsh economic environment of the past several years, many people have had to uproot their families and relocate to different parts of the country to find jobs. Still other people have chosen for various reasons to move away from their hometown roots. In the process, these people often have left behind elderly parents, who may have few or no other relatives to look after them.

While these elderly people may have doctors, nurses, and lawyers to handle their medical and legal needs, they may not have anyone to help out with day-to-day chores and errands, and they may need someone to take or accompany them to the doctor's or lawyer's office. This presents an opportunity for a freelancer who enjoys working with elderly people and is committed to providing a service or variety of services.

In this case, a freelancer would have to be somewhat of a generalist, because the services could range from simply picking up a prescription at the pharmacy to helping a person fill out routine paperwork to fixing—or arranging the repair of—a kitchen appliance. If the elderly person or couple still lives in the family home, then there may be some yard work, gutter cleaning, and general maintenance work to do. If you don't do this yourself, you at least need to be able to hire people for specific jobs and coordinate their work with your clients' schedules.

Typical first steps and considerations

o Determine what services you can do and what type of fee structure to use in billing clients.

o Compile your specialized phone book, including the names and numbers of pharmacists, appliance-repair services, plumbers, carpenters, lawn-care services, and local handyman services.

o Talk to the pharmacists, doctors, lawyers, mechanics, and others you listed in the above phone book and ask them if they know of elderly people in need of your services.

o Make some calls to potential customers, or potential customers' relatives, to determine if they are interested in your services.

Typical requirements

o A well-rounded knowledge of your community, such as what services and government agencies are located there, where the medical offices and pharmacies are, and who provides what specialized service.

o A telephone with voice mail or an answering device, preferably a phone that is not answered by your children, unless they have been trained to answer it in a businesslike manner.

o A reliable vehicle to drive. This can be anything from a small compact car to a pickup truck, depending on whether your services include home maintenance.

o An information system, such as a computer and database program, that keeps track of your clients' special needs or circumstances and gives you immediate access to the information in case of urgent calls.

Furniture Restorer/Refinisher

A wood table that has had a few too many cold drinks set down on it without benefit of a coaster, a metal plant stand that has been scratched and dented over the course of five household moves in eight years: These two pieces are not antiques ready for donation to the museum, but neither are they pieces of junk ready for the dumpster. They're just household furniture in need of a refinisher. This function can be combined with upholstery and full antique restoration to form a multiple-level home-based business. You can also buy some pieces at yard sales, estate sales, or flea markets; perform your refinishing/restoration magic on them; and then sell them for a profit to add another dimension to your business.

Typical first steps and considerations

○ Determine what local regulations apply to disposal of stripping and finishing chemicals.

○ Visit some antiques shops to determine the potential for jobs from them and from their clients.

○ Talk to nearby woodworkers, metalworkers, and other crafts people. They often get inquiries from their own clients looking for referrals on refinishing and restoration. Also, they may have upholstery work to subcontract.

Typical requirements

○ A shop that is environmentally and personally safe and that complies with local zoning laws.

○ A supply of pertinent chemicals and proper tools.

○ A reliable vehicle to transport pieces to and from your shop.

Videographer

While a growing number of American families own their own video cameras, not everyone can shoot good, professional footage, much less edit a lot of footage into one coherent tape. The market for a professional video photographer can range from documentation of someone's possessions for insurance purposes to filming family reunions to filming weddings to making a full sales or training program for a corporate

client. If a videographer teams up with a writer, then the possibilities multiply.

Typical first steps and considerations

○ Assess your technical abilities and determine whether you can provide some or all of the above-mentioned services. You may have to take some of the less-glamorous jobs before you can limit your activities to a specialty, but if you can specialize, you can bring in a higher hourly rate of pay.

○ Talk to other video service providers, video supply retailers, still photographers, or anyone familiar with the field to determine whether there is a market for what you want to do. The market may be wide open or already saturated with underworked videographers. If the latter is the case, then look for a niche that isn't being serviced. There also may be subcontract work available from already established businesses.

○ Produce your own video presentation of your business. You may even want to produce a short version that can be mailed to prospective clients and a longer version that you present in person. Incorporate both your resume and the services you offer into the presentation.

Typical requirements

○ A video camera of sufficient quality to perform your work reliably. But you'll also need one or more backup cameras, plus sufficient lighting equipment for your specialties.

o Videotape editing equipment.

o To produce sophisticated presentations, you will need computer hardware and software that enable you to incorporate animation and text matter in your work.

o A working space large enough to allow for some in-house filming for product shots, close-up photography, or video portraits.

Woodworker

Advancements in technology have caused major changes within the business of woodworking, in terms of the availability of sophisticated tools, computer-aided design programs, and the integration of computerized instructions into the operation of such tools as lathes. But the beauty of woodworking is that you can be either a modern woodworker, using all these advanced tools, or you can be a traditional woodworker, using mostly old-fashioned hand tools. Demand exists for products from both types of woodworkers. The biggest difference comes in start-up costs, with computer-operated equipment running into the tens of thousands of dollars and the traditional tools totaling just in the thousands for a small home wood shop. It's the latter proposition that will be discussed here.

Typical first steps and considerations

o Analyze and assess your skills as a woodworker and determine what products and what level of craftsmanship you want to provide your customers.

o Develop dependable sources of supply, including lumber dealers, tool dealers, and woodworkers' supply houses. It's a good idea to have more than one source for lumber, since it is a commodity item and highly vulnerable to constant shifts in the marketplace.

o Develop a customer base by talking to other professional and part-time woodworkers, local furniture dealers, the local high school or community shop teacher, or anyone who may have knowledge of people looking for original works in wood. Craft galleries and high-end furniture galleries also are good sources of information. Visit a craft show and survey the woodworking booths.

o Set up your business to best fit your individual capabilities to the existing market.

Typical requirements

o Tools are about as personal to the woodworker as notebooks are to a news reporter. Every shop will be set up somewhat differently. But there are some basic tools that can be considered essential, including a table saw or radial arm saw, band saw, planer, drill and/or drill press, router, circular saw, and sander. Depending on your specialty (carving, turning, cabinet-making), you will need additional tools such as chisels and gouges, lathes, and grinders. You also will need design and incidental tools, such as rulers, calipers and clamps.

o A shop that is big enough for your setup, isolated or soundproofed so as not to bother family and neighbors, and legal enough for the local zoning enforcement officer.

o A record-keeping system that not only helps you keep track of income and expenses, but specific details of jobs, such as design specifications, customizing details, materials costs, and time invested.

Writing and Editorial Services

Writing is not a computer-dependent occupation. Neither is editing. But if you expect to make it as a freelance writer or editor in today's world, your writing and editing business has to be conducted on a computer. Schedules are short, budgets are tight, and no time exists anymore for the writer who has to write something out by hand, transpose it to a typewriter, and send it to a publisher on 20-lb white bond paper.

Various publishers request that manuscripts be submitted in various forms, but you're likely to be asked to submit both a hard copy and a computer-disk version of whatever you write, whether it's a book or a magazine article. Another preferred method of transmitting articles and book chapters is via computer, either from computer to computer through a direct connection or a bulletin-board system, or over a network, using electronic mail (e-mail) or electronic file transfer.

Typical first steps and considerations

o Determine what you want to write. Anything that makes money, right? That's a natural inclination and a good survival strategy, but not a good long-term solution. Writers who are used to seeing their work published quickly and who need that fast reward might not do well as book authors. And a writer who is used to the longer, more planned schedules of book writing might not be satisfied with a piece that has to be turned around in five to seven days, or less. And some writers are best at handling quick-turnaround work for daily and weekly publications, public-relations agencies, corporate communications departments, or individual clients.

o Develop a list of clients for whom you can produce work.

o Develop a list of ideas long enough to withstand numerous rejections and deletions.

o Draw up a schedule, including starting dates and deadlines, and take a realistic look at whether you can do everything that is required on deadline.

Typical requirements

o If budget is a major consideration, you can get an electronic word processor that is a combination type-writer, electronic monitor, and printer. But make sure it has the capability of saving files to a floppy disk that can be read by a computer.

o But for not much more money, you can get an entry-level computer system. This is still a tricky maneuver, however, since you have to decide whether to buy a Macintosh or IBM-compatible system. While the compatibility gap between the two operating systems is narrower than it was just a few years ago, you would be better off getting the system that matches your best and regular clients.

You'll also need a modem and a laser or ink-jet printer.

o A fax machine, or the capability to send and receive faxes through your computer with a fax modem.

o A subscription to an on-line computer service, such as CompuServe or America On Line, or an Internet connection.

o An office area with enough room and isolation to allow you to work peacefully, use the telephone effectively, and leave your work in progress in such a way that it doesn't take you a half hour to get set up each time you start to write.

PART TWO

WHO ARE FREELANCERS?

CHAPTER THREE

On the Fence But Ready to Jump: Are You a Freelancer?

KEY TERMS

discipline   *experience*
juggler   *self-confidence*

A freelancer is a business person, a dreamer, a gambler, a family person, a loner, a thinker, a pragmatist, an idealist, and a **juggler**–possibly, more juggler than anything else. How else can you reconcile all those other concepts into one person?

To take the definition a little further, there are natural freelancers, willing freelancers, anxious freelancers, frustrated freelancers, and reluctant freelancers. In other words, some freelancers are freelancers of their own free will, while others are freelancers because of circumstances. Photographers, artists, and writers are often natural freelancers who are quite comfortable going from assignment to assignment, publication to publication, craft show to craft show. At the other end of the spectrum, a recently laid-off executive might be a reluctant freelancer, because the only option available to make money presently is to market his or her expertise as a consultant.

Who are the newest types of freelancers?

O Retirees looking for second careers, perhaps less structured than their first

O Women who come up against stubborn traditions and glass ceilings and who advance further and faster working for themselves o Midlevel, even top-level, executives who found few corporate job opportunities when they were laid off

o Women and men who are new parents who decide to work at home, bringing their professions and their parenting more in line with each other

Regardless of your status, you wouldn't be reading this book if you weren't at least thinking about freelancing as a work style and life-style or already doing it. Being your own boss has a definite attraction for some people. Quite often, these people just want to take more control of their lives and destinies. Accumulation of money is often less of a goal than being able to watch a son or daughter play in a school basketball game on a weekday afternoon.

Chief Qualities Of Freelancers

If you're already a freelancer at least part-time, you have a good idea about what it takes to succeed. But you may be among the many people who are on the verge of becoming freelancers, who wonder whether they possess the right attributes to survive the business, much less succeed. Freelancers embody many characteristics, especially self-confidence.

But freelancers also are:

o professionally ambitious

o experienced

o self-motivated

o self-starting

o results-oriented

o tenacious

o independent

If they're successful, they know how to run a business, too.

Experience plays a major role in a freelancer's success. Sure, you can freelance while going to college and gain knowledge and contacts that you will use later on. But serious freelancing, the kind that pays the bills and sends your kids to college, only comes from honing your skills and interacting with associates and colleagues for a period of time. Experience manifests itself in many ways, including how you make decisions. It is sometimes synonymous with professionalism. Some examples of experience:

o An advertising consultant insisting diplomatically but successfully that his egotistical client lower his chin so that he doesn't come off quite as egotistical when he appears in his own television commercial.

o A computer consultant knowing that there are at least two ways to perform any function on the computer, and if one way doesn't work, it doesn't mean it can't be done.

o A furniture restorer knowing when to recommend to a client that a fragile heirloom chair should be put into storage and not used, rather than restored and put back into the living room. The furniture restorer will lose some immediate business but likely will gain the trust and future business of the client.

THE PAJAMAS TEST

Do phrases such as "the clothes make the person" bother you? Can you work effectively sitting in front of your computer at 3:00 a.m., wearing frayed $15 pajamas? Some people can work in their pajamas, but others prefer to sleep in them. Most clients would prefer that you do the latter if you're meeting with them.

What does this have to do with business? You have to consider such things before sinking savings, time, and possibly a career into such a volatile work style as freelancing. The pajamas are only a symbol of such profound concepts as work habits, professional attitudes, client perceptions, and self-confidence—things that, if you worry about them too much, can keep you awake at night.

Home-based workers do not have to worry about a dress code, but many people associate work with certain types of clothes and cannot perform well if they're not dressed for work. But freelancers have to perform under a variety of conditions, often on tight deadlines that require you to burn some 3:00 a.m. oil to get a product to a client at 9:00 a.m. sharp.

When you're a freelancer, you might not have to worry about what a manager thinks of your performance, attire, and attitude before deciding whether to give you a 3 percent raise after a year's hard work. But if that manager also has the decision-making authority to assign work to independent contractors, you have to consider whether the manager perceives that you will perform the work competently, on time, and without requesting more money.

The question then becomes not whether you show up for a business meeting in your pajamas—hopefully you won't—but whether you feel confident and comfortable enough with yourself to perform the work and deliver the final product or service on time and within budget. If you take a relaxed attitude to match the frayed pajama sleeves, then the deadline may sneak up on you. But if you can work hard and effectively in pajamas when you have to, then you have a chance as a freelancer.

How do you feel about wearing a fashionable business suit to a "power" office meeting at 3:00 p.m. "downtown," especially if you have to avoid wrinkling the suit while walking and sweating six blocks in 97-degree heat? Working for a big corporation, you may have been one of two types of employees: someone who managed to stay in the shadows and let other people handle things or someone who thrived on such meetings and let other people stay back and fill in the details. As a freelancer, you have to be both people. You have to get the business by presenting yourself in the proper image, then do the work by executing your skills professionally and tediously.

o A woodworker knowing that the species of wood the customer wants will not hold up as a tabletop and recommending other species that will be more suitable in terms of appearance, stability, and workability.

o A writer knowing that, even after years of studying and writing about a subject, he still has to catch up on the latest research before he can write about it again.

How long do you have to work for someone else before you are experienced enough to go it alone? That question brings up another significant quality for a freelancer: self-reliance. There is no formula for determining how long—or whether—you have to work for someone else before you can venture forth as a freelancer. You have to rely on your own judgment, which, hopefully, will be based on a sound knowledge of your craft and your market. A common freelancer today is a woman who is taking a break from the professional world for a few years to stay at home with her children. Previously, she may have been an accountant, a teacher, or an editor. Now she wants to build up a home-based freelance business based on her background.

Confident, Yet...

One important mark of a freelancer is that he or she is self-confident. How else can you put your life, and the lives of your family members, on the financial line? The **self-confidence** generally comes from knowledge, competence, and experience working in a particular field.

The computer consultant who spent 15 years developing systems and applications for a major corporation knows he has something to offer both his former employer and newfound clients when he starts his own company. The editor who managed the work flow of a growing monthly magazine for 10 years knows she can analyze a client's communications needs and coordinate a successful newsletter and press-relations campaign. A woodworker knows she can make top-quality art furniture pieces because she's been doing it for years.

In this sense, the simplest job for a freelancer is doing the actual work. Now comes the hardest part: getting and keeping the work. This is where the freelancer's self-confidence can erode into a neurosis. A common fear is not getting the first client, but that fear is often allayed by the fact that many freelancers pick up immediate business from former employers. The next fear is not having enough business to keep the cash flowing, and a common reaction to that fear is to take on too much work. Then, you either miss deadlines, work so hard that you burn out, or both.

Here comes the juggler in you again. You have to juggle being an expert and a marketer of your expertise with your work schedule and personal obligations. In the process, hopefully you can whittle the freelancing forest down to a tree branch, carving out the types of work you want to do. That would be the work you do best and the work that eventually pays best because of your expertise.

UP FRONT UNDERSTANDINGS

Freelancers must be able to focus their minds and keep them focused on the overall picture, while still taking care of the daily details of work and life. One way to do that is to make a pact with yourself up front, before you quit your day job. Here's a simple pact that can apply to any freelance occupation.

I have to run a business. In the process...

I have to work hard

I have to know my market

I have to sell to my market

I have to deliver to my market

I have to collect from my market

I have to make a profit

Ability to Size Yourself Up

One critical characteristic for free-lancers is that they have to be honest with themselves when it is time to assess whether they can succeed on their own. In some respects, this is easy. You don't have to make up excuses any more about traffic jams causing you to get back late from lunch. But when it's time for you to take a look at yourself and your potential in a freelancing business, you'll have to admit that it's not traffic that causes you to get back late from lunch, but your own lack of **discipline.** Perhaps you will regain that discipline once you're on your own, but it's an issue worth contemplating now.

FREELANCERS, A–Z

The various types of freelancing occupations bring in equally various levels of income. Also, the degree of special skills required for freelancing runs the gamut from basic to highly specialized. Here's an alphabetical list of possible jobs for freelancers:

accountant – advertising agent, consultant – animal breeder – antiques broker, consultant – appliance repair serviceperson – appraiser – artist – baker – bookkeeper – book producer – bridal and wedding consultant – candle maker – caterer – children's lunch-box service operator – children's party planner – cleaning service operator – closet designer – computer bulletin-board service operator – computer consultant – copywriter – craft artisan – designer – desktop publisher – direct-mail advertiser – dollhouse maker – editor – elderly assistance provider – environmental consultant – errand service operator – export/import broker – food service provider – furniture maker, furniture restorer/refinisher – gardening consultant – groomer (pets) – guidebook publisher – home-based business consultant – home maintenance service operator – illustrator – interior decorator – janitor – journalist – knitter – literary agent – lunch caterer – maid service operator – management consultant – marketing consultant – musician, music teacher – news-clipping service operator – office services provider – organizer – painter – pet-care provider – photographer – plant service operator – potter – proofreader – publisher – quilter – reading tutor – recreation planner – researcher – sandwich maker – secretarial services operator – sewing business operator – shopping service operator – taxidermist – tax preparer – toy maker – translator – trophy maker, trophy service operator – upholsterer –videographer – woodworker – writer – xylographer – xylophonist – yard and lawn-care specialist – yoga instructor – zoology tutor

Honesty extends to more than just self-discipline, of course. It also applies to your ability to size up your work habits, commitments, responsibilities, attitudes toward people, and resilience in the face of rejection and other setbacks. A few questions to ask yourself:

o Would I hire me if I were looking for an independent contractor for a short-term project? Why? Why not?

o Once I get that first big contract, will I put off getting started on it (and jeopardize my future), because I have some perceived freedom and some advance money in the bank?

o Am I overcommitted financially right now to the point that I can't forgo a steady cash flow?

o Am I sufficiently committed to my chosen occupation that I'll want to do it even though it doesn't bring in any cash for a period of time?

o Do I "like people" well enough to sometimes put aside personal feelings to gain professional work?

o Am I strong enough to withstand the rejection from one client, then make an appointment immediately with another client to make up for the loss?

CHAPTER FOUR

It's a Lonely World, But You're Not Alone

KEY TERMS

contacts
isolation
Schedule C

electronic mail
networking
trade associations

While working as a freelancer in your home office or workshop, you may feel—and you'll definitely have to overcome—a sense of isolation. But you're definitely not alone. The number of people working part-time or full-time for themselves increased dramatically between 1980 and 1990, and the growth in self-employment has been steady since then. It is impossible to pinpoint exactly how many freelancers work out of their homes in the United States. Different federal agencies keep various statistics, and not all freelancers and self-employed people fall under the same statistical definitions.

The figures bandied about in newspaper and magazine articles—12 million, 15 million, 20 million, 40 million—can get somewhat confusing. The figures are supplied primarily by two government agencies or by commercial research companies, who sell their reports to big corporations that want to sell products to home-based workers. On the surface, it looks like there are conflicting numbers, and in some cases there are. But usually, it's just a matter of interpretation and analysis, of deciding which statistics relate to which definitions.

To simplify matters, a few categories are defined as they relate to this chapter:

○ *Home-based worker* can be either a self-employed person or a wage or salary employee who works at home, such as a telecommuter. The largest figures published about home offices apply to both of these categories.

○ *Self-employed* means you run your own business, whether it is a retail store, a muffler shop, or a home-based consulting service. This category would relate to the midrange figures published. Freelancers are included in this category, but so are owners of retail stores at the mall. It can also mean, by some definitions, either incorporated or unincorporated businesses (see Chapter 9). But for tax-filing purposes, if you're incorporated, you're an employee of the corporation.

○ *Home-based business,* however, has a purer definition. This is where many freelancers fit in, as operators of a business managed from home. This category, too, could refer to incorporated or unincorporated businesses, but typically it refers to the latter. This would relate to the lower-range published figures.

You're One in a Million... Five Million... Twelve Million...

One good way to tell how many people are freelancing is to look at the number of people who file a **Schedule C** with their federal income tax returns. This is the form on which you report income or losses from a sole proprietor-ship. According to the Internal Revenue Service (IRS), the number of people filing Schedule C forms increased from 8.9 million in 1980 to 11.9 million in 1985 to 14.6 million in 1990. Preliminary figures indicate that 15.3 million people filed a Schedule C in 1992. That amounts to a 72 percent increase in the number of people who filed Schedule C over a 12-year period.

Another federal agency, the U.S. Bureau of Labor Statistics (BLS), publishes a monthly *Current Population Survey* (CPS) that gathers research on various characteristics of the U.S. labor force. The survey is conducted for BLS by the Bureau of the Census and involves about 60,000 households. Analysts and economists use the survey as a basis for articles in labor-oriented publications.

An article entitled "Who Are the Self-Employed? Employment Profiles and Recent Trends" by George T. Silvestri, published in the spring 1991 issue of *Occupational Outlook Quarterly*, pegged the total number of self-employed in 1990 at 15.6 million, including 10 million who owned unincorporated businesses, 3.5 million who owned incorporated businesses, and 2 million who held wage or hourly jobs and worked part-time for themselves, also. More than half of the unincorporated self-employed worked in service-related and retail occupations.

Home-based workers were analyzed in the article "Work at Home: Data from the CPS" by William G. Deming, published in the February 1994 issue of *Monthly Labor Review*. Based on the May 1991 CPS survey, the latest that relates to home-based self-employment, the article

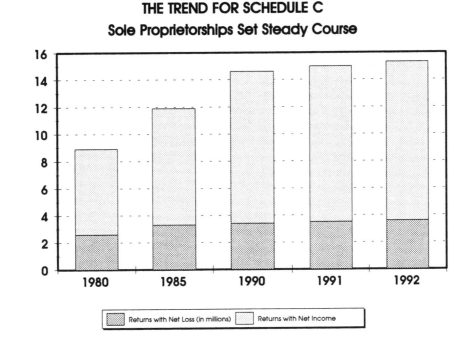

THE TREND FOR SCHEDULE C
Sole Proprietorships Set Steady Course

Returns with Net Loss (in millions)   Returns with Net Income

Source: Internal Revenue Service

The number of people filing Schedule Cs increased from 8.9 million in 1980 to an estimated 15.3 million in 1992.

noted that 20 million people did some job-related work at home, but only about 7.4 million were paid for it. Of those, 5.6 million were self-employed people working at home. About 20 percent of them worked at home 35 hours or more per week (full-time), and 55 percent worked at home more than 8 hours per week (part-time). In calculating the numbers, however, the survey lumped together both the incorporated and the unincorporated self-employed, so these numbers cannot be statistically compared with the number of Schedule C filers.

Recent projections and estimates by the government, commercial researchers, and trade associations indicate that the number of self-employed people was more than 20 million in 1994, and 41 million or more people may have been working at home. Estimates for the number of home-based businesses range from 12 million to 24 million.

Whatever the true number may be, in many ways the trend toward home-based businesses is a reflection of a society coming full circle to its Colonial roots. In Colonial times, most businesses, even retail stores, were run from the home. But the Industrial Revolution started a movement that took people out of homes and into factories and offices. Now, with technology so advanced that you can equip a home office much like a central business office and stay in touch virtually

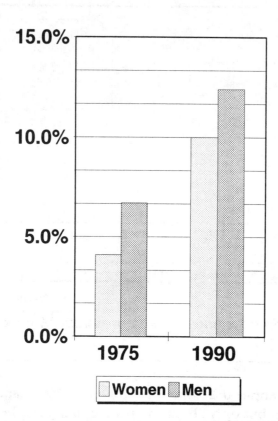

GROWTH IN SELF-EMPLOYMENT* FOR WOMEN AND MEN, 1975–1990

Source: U.S. Bureau of Labor Statistics

The rate of self-employment is determined by calculating the percentage of self-employed people in the total work force.

anywhere, any time, the tide is coming back in.

Freelancing Isn't Gender-Specific

Freelancers come in all sizes, shapes, and ages and, of course, in both genders. That's one of the attractions of freelancing. You don't have a weight limit, as

jockeys do. You don't have an age limit, as commercial airline pilots do. And even though many gender barriers crumbled over the past two decades, there still are some gender gaps, not to mention glass ceilings, for women in many occupational categories.

According to the 1990 BLS profile of the self-employed, women represented about one-third of the 10 million unincorporated business owners. This showed an increase from about one-quarter in 1975. However, the 1991 BLS survey found that men and women were almost equally likely to be home-based freelancers. In raw numbers, men slightly outnumbered women in the part-time category and in moonlighting, or working a second job in addition to a primary full-time job. Women, however, were more likely to be working in full-time home-based enterprises.

"Characteristics of Self-Employed Women in the United States" by Theresa J. Devine, in the March 1994 issue of *Monthly Labor Review,* cited women as a fast-growing segment of the self-employed. In 1975, the percentage of working women who were self-employed amounted to 4.1 percent. This number grew to 6.7 percent in 1990, a 63 percent increase in the rate of self-employment for women over a 15-year period.

Men during this period accounted for more self-employed people, but they had a lower rate of growth. In 1975, 10 percent of working men were self-employed. This grew to 12.4 percent in 1990, a 24 percent increase in the rate of self-employment. These figures relate to nonagricultural occupations only and apply only to unincorporated businesses.

The BLS surveys indicate that freelancing from home typically takes place after people have some experience under their belts. According to the 1991 survey, the largest category of home-based workers was the 35–44 age group; the next largest, the 45–54 age group; and the third largest, the 25–34 age group.

Working Alone, But Staying Connected

It's ironic that freelancers often choose to work alone because they want their independence. Because this independence, in the form of **isolation,** is also a threat to their survival. While some freelancers thrive on isolation, others flounder in it. Overall, it's probably more of a problem than a benefit, so having a network of associates, friends, and acquaintances helps to overcome it.

As a freelancer, you'll have to define for yourself how much **networking** you'll have to do to both stay in business and stay sane. Networking is just the modern-day word for communicating, or exchanging information, with individuals and companies.

There was no need for networking in previous, less-mobile societies. Men used to graduate from high school; go to college or the military or both; then come home, go to work, and raise a family. Their employers already knew who they were and who their families were. This was sometimes an advantage, sometimes a disadvantage. Women were even more confined in their roles until the women's movement began to open up new opportunities in the 1960s.

As technology advanced, the world got smaller, and people became much more mobile. Today, you can't depend on a family friend or your dad's employer to help you find a job. You have to build your own network of **contacts.** This is true whether you plan to work in traditional wage and hourly occupations or as a freelancer. If you've been building up your skills and profession working for

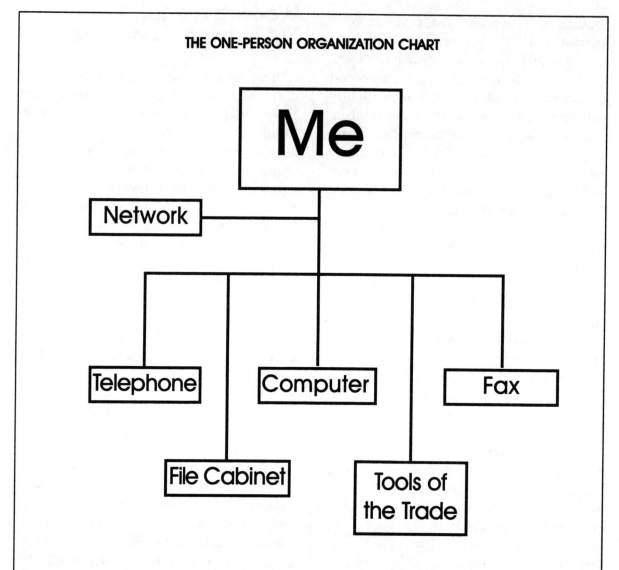

THE ONE-PERSON ORGANIZATION CHART

Me

Network

Telephone

Computer

Fax

File Cabinet

Tools of the Trade

Just because you're a one-person business, it doesn't mean you don't have an organizational structure. You can think of items such as your telephone and computer as your assistants and your network of business associates and friends as your board of advisors.

regular employers for a period of years, you probably already have at least the beginning of your own network of profession-related contacts. Now, you just have to supplement that with business-related contacts.

Networking means more than just business contacts for freelancers, however. It means having someone to talk to about common everyday issues related to working at home alone. It means having someone to honestly critique a new marketing concept you just thought of. And it means being ready yourself to listen to others' problems and victories, to have a sense of sharing with and learning from others.

Probably the easiest way to stay connected is to join a home-based-business association. If one doesn't exist in your area, then perhaps it's time for you to start one—as if you didn't have enough on your calendar already. There are quite a few home-based-business associations active around the country. The American Association of Home-Based Businesses in Rockville, Maryland, is one place to start if you need help finding a group or starting your own. You can also get a directory of home-based businesses by subscribing to the "Working from Home" forum on CompuServe.

It might also be good to join just a business group, without regard to whether its focus is home offices or not. Chambers of commerce, **trade associations,** or other groups can not only introduce you to people with whom you can talk, but they can also open up new market possibilities.

Just remember that your time is a great asset, so try to pick the organization or group that best fits your individual needs.

If your business derives most of its income from local sources, joining a local civic club can be beneficial. People are always more willing to do business with someone they know, someone they see regularly at a monthly club luncheon, than with someone who limits his or her outside visits to either sales calls or personal errands. Getting involved in special committees of the civic club, such as working on the food committee for a summer outdoor festival, can put you in touch with people who either share common interests or can possibly use your services.

In summary, your network should provide you with three benefits:

o Contacts with whom you can discuss common professional problems, issues, and benefits

o Contacts that may yield direct business

o Contacts that may yield indirect business, either through referrals or subcontracts

Connecting the Modern Way: E-mail and Life On the "Highway"

Another way to network is to do it in the technical sense—over one of the online computer services. You've no doubt seen, heard, or read about the so-called Information Superhighway. Typically, this refers to the Internet, a global network of networks that got its start as a government and academic network but has rapidly become accessible to and used by common individuals and businesses. But the Internet is just the beginning for the bigger information superhighway concept, which will blend computers, televisions, and telephones into one integrated information center for the home and business.

The Internet is a fantastic source of information and an excellent method of communicating by **electronic mail,** or e-mail. But there are other options, also, that may be more user-friendly to people who are not accustomed to operating on-line. These include CompuServe, America Online, Prodigy, and GEnie. The costs can vary for each service from a few dollars to $50, $75, or more per month, depending on which service you choose and how much you use it for such things as research and downloading of software.

You can use on-line services to send e-mail quickly and efficiently to anyone else who is also on-line. On the Internet, for instance, you can send a short message to a professor in Australia, or one in Bulgaria, requesting information that he or she is better able to provide than anyone else in the world. Or you may just want to send a request across town or to the next city confirming an appointment for the next day.

The price of either e-mail message is included in your monthly bill, and it doesn't cost any more to send the message to Australia than it does to send it two blocks away.

You can also participate in ongoing on-line discussions about any number of topics, including home-based businesses. On CompuServe, for instance, the "Working From Home" forum is a computerized meeting place for people who run home businesses or are interested in doing so. And on the Internet, a wide variety of "usenet" groups exist, in which specific areas of interest, such as biotechnology or geography, are discussed by people around the world.

The number of people participating in on-line conversations and in e-mail is growing every day. You might be surprised at the number of messages you get just as a result of putting your e-mail address on your business card and letterhead.

PART THREE

WHEN IS IT TIME TO FREELANCE?

CHAPTER FIVE

The Time to Go for It

KEY TERMS

competition

seasonal fluctuations

energy level

start-up seminar

Once the personal decisions have been made to go into freelancing or to expand an existing freelancing business, you'll have to consider timing. Is the time right for you? Is there really a big enough market for your product or service, and is the market ready for another supplier? What kind of financial plan do you have in place? Is the health insurance and business insurance arranged? Is your business plan sound?

Timing is critical in business. But it is not an exact science. It's more an art form. It involves being knowledgeable about not only your business, but also the overall economy and your special market. And it involves some gut decisions on your part, gut decisions based on your own research and considerations. Timing is more critical if you're unemployed, because you don't have as many options as someone with a steady income does, and you also have to decide when to stop looking for another job and start being your own boss.

Dreams Have a Way Of Turning into Reality

If you've dreamed about being a free-lancer, and you think you will thrive professionally and financially as your own boss, then you probably are a good freelancing candidate. To succeed as a freelancer, you have to believe in yourself and have a positive outlook. But if you're not careful, you'll find that dreams have a way of turning into nightmares—especially if in pursuing your dream, you ignore the realities of marketing, economics, and finance. Freelancing is more business than dream. And business depends on such things as preparation and timing to be successful.

Following are some basic questions to ask yourself. They will help you determine whether you are ready to make the leap into full-time freelancing. Other important issues, such as those relating to finances and record keeping, are covered in more detail in Chapter 10. Hopefully, you won't embark upon your venture before reading further.

Questions to ask yourself now:

How much longer can I do what I'm doing?

Are you unhappy at your present job? Or do you like what you're doing, but is your job in danger of being eliminated? If you are unhappy where you are working, what are the consequences if you stay? Will you lose your ambition? If your boss gets fired (not uncommon in today's corporate world), will you be happy? If you like your job but are afraid you might lose it, what are your options? Can you find comparable work elsewhere? If you keep coming up with dead ends, then it's time to at least think about and plan for freelancing. But if you keep coming up with "well, maybe...," then you need to think about other options a little longer.

Do I have enough business lined up to keep me in work for six months or more?

This is a matter of judgment. Six months at the pace you've been working may be longer or shorter than six months at the pace you'll work as a freelancer. Some considerations include whether you will have to subcontract any of your work to others to make up for the lack of support from other departments, whether you will finish a job sooner because you don't have to attend all those two-hour staff meetings any more, and whether you have accurately estimated the time needed to complete the work.

Is the business I have scheduled safe and reliable in terms of when I will get paid?

Freelancing, as mentioned before, is a volatile business. Clients change their minds and their schedules, cut expenses, go out of business, or just don't pay fast enough. Getting an agreement in writing helps, but make sure there's a clause that deals with delays in the schedule and changes in the scope of the work that you're hired to do.

Do I have enough money in the bank to last six months, a year, two years—until I can make a steady income from the business?

Here again, it's difficult to estimate, because switching from a salary to a freelance income can change every part of your life—how you eat, how you entertain yourself and your family, how much gas you use in your car, and how often you go to the doctor (see next question). Plan where you could cut the family budget if you had to.

Do I have adequate health insurance?

This is a biggie. Obtaining catastrophic health insurance isn't usually a problem, but what about coverage for doctors' visits? How often do you go now, and who pays? If you belong to a health maintenance organization (HMO), and you've been paying $5–$10 each time you visit the doctor because of sniffles, you may not go as often when you convert to a high-deductible conventional insurance plan. And don't forget about disability insurance in case an injury or illness prevents you from working.

Is my family ready for me to do this?

Running a freelance business is difficult enough without having to deal with domestic problems as well. Discuss everything up front with your family, including both financial and personal issues.

Do I have the energy to run a business right now?

Take stock of your personal health. Becoming a freelancer and your own boss can be invigorating, spurring you to new levels of creativity and insight. But it can also bring you down very fast, because you not only have to perform your work, you have to market it and manage it, too. Your **energy level** is important.

Am I ready to give up the camaraderie of coworkers and spend my time alone with just the phone, fax, four walls, and the cat?

The problem of isolation for freelancers cannot be overemphasized. Take a few days off and spend them "working" in your home office before you quit your day job to see how you fare.

When the Market Will Bear It

In marketing, a phrase often heard when setting price is, "What the market will bear." This marketing concept can mean negative or positive things for your business. If you produce a certain product, you need to sell it at a price that covers the cost, overhead, and profit. But if a thousand other people are selling the same thing cheaper, then you have to sell your product for the price established by the market—or find another product to sell. On the other hand, if your product is a one-of-a-kind item in high demand, you can sell it at a premium price because the market is open and receptive. The key word here is market. What is yours, and what will it bear?

Knowing your market and analyzing the strengths and weaknesses of the **competition** can help you decide when to go into business. If you know who your competitors are, what they are doing, and when, sooner or later you will see an opening for yourself. Once you're in business, keeping a watch on your competitors will help you hone your marketing skills and will keep you on your toes when it comes to the quality of your work.

One of the oldest methods of investigating competitors is to be—or pretend to be—a customer of theirs. This is more difficult for some occupations than for others. Typically, the more specialized you are, the more difficult it is to pretend.

If you are contemplating going into desktop publishing, for instance, you can call around or visit area shops that advertise such services and say you need to get business cards or letterhead printed. That's the kind of call anyone in this business would expect. While you're talking with the shop owners or managers, you can ask about their other capabilities and how they price jobs, duly taking note of how they handle customers, too. You can explore the possibility of a brochure or regular newsletter, taking notes on the type of equipment that would be used and what the delivery schedule would be. If the shop says it is going to expand soon, then you may have to move quickly into your own operation, or you may want to wait and see what that other shop does.

But if you're going to start your own computer-consulting business, in which you specialize in designing custom software for medium-sized to large corporations, sizing up the competition is a little more difficult. Here, you have to be aware of regional, state, and national trends in both business and computers. You have to know who your competitors or prospective competitors are, a task that's not always as easy as identifying print shops by leafing through the yellow pages. You will have to depend mostly on your own network of associates and business acquaintances to provide you with information, and it would be impossible to pretend to be a customer with them.

Some of the things you'll need to know about your competitors:

o *What they do.*

What kinds of products/services do they offer?

o *For whom.*
Who are their customers or clients?

o *When they do it.*

What are their operating hours? What is their turnaround time on particular jobs?

o *Where they do it.*

Do they, too, operate from home? If not, will they have an advantage over you by being located in a commercial building? Also, what is the extent of their market geographically?

o *How they do it.*

How do they produce their product? How is the quality of their work? How do they sell their product?

o *Why they do it.*

This may not be obvious. Some starting points: Are they overtly happy and pleasant when you visit their business? Do they approach their work with zeal, or can you tell the only reason they're there is because they inherited the firm from Uncle David?

o *How much they do.*

Are they constantly, or hardly, busy? Do they always have a backlog of work?

o *How much they make doing it.*

Again, this may not be obvious. Good indicators are their life-style and the kinds of cars they drive. But, of course, this is only a rough estimate.

○ *How their customers feel about them.*

Do people around town mention their name anytime there is a discussion about the product or service they provide? Do their customers perceive them to be the best in the business? Or is someone complaining every time you visit their business?

From this information, you can develop your own list of comparisons between what your competitor offers and what you plan to offer. After that, you can decide if the time is right to plunge ahead, if you need to wait a while, or if you need to enter the market on a part-time basis and build from there. If your competitor has a newsletter or brochure, pick it up and take it home for reference. Also, analyze the competitor's advertising. It's often an indication of current trends in products and pricing. Then, see if the company is living up to its advertising. If it isn't, maybe it's time for you to go into the market.

Going from Part-Time To Full-Time

The transition from part-time freelancer to full-time freelancer can be tricky. Especially if you have settled into a schedule of work that is impossible to maintain and still hold on to your family and social life, like working full-time for someone else and part-time for yourself.

In most ways, however, you still have to go through the same steps as others who are starting anew when you decide to take a hobby or part-time business full-time.

Some of the considerations involved in this shift include whether to increase your prices to bring in more money, whether to upgrade your computer hardware and software to handle more work, and whether to expand your work space to accommodate 12-hour days instead of 2- or 3-hour sessions.

Another major consideration is having your freelance income change from being a part of your budget to being all of your budget. Have you saved all the income you've made as a part-timer and lived only on the salaried income? Or have you needed the part-time income to help pay the bills? If the latter is the case, you'll have to cut expenses and plan your transition to full-time freelancing very carefully.

Consider the Seasonal Aspects

You may have to consider **seasonal fluctuations** in business when timing your start-up, particularly if your product or service is sold to the general public. Typically, you want to start your venture just before the busiest time of the year, so income will start to flow in right away. The disadvantage of this is that you have to be well prepared to handle the rush. If you have enough money in the bank to forgo business income for a while, you may want to start during a slow season to build up your reputation for quality and organize your working habits.

More about marketing is contained in Chapter 11, but some examples of seasonal considerations follow:

○ If your specialty is pet care, including operating an on-site pet-sitting service and an off-site pet-visiting service, your busiest time is likely to be summer, when most people take vacations.

○ If you are a caterer who specializes in children's menus, late August and September could be a busy time. You could develop a lunch-box service, in which you package lunches in insulated pouches and deliver them to children's homes before school, exchanging the pouches in much the same way as milkmen used to exchange glass milk bottles.

○ If you're a craft artisan who depends on craft shows for income, your year is probably divided into selling seasons and making seasons. You make things in the summer and winter, then sell them in the spring and fall, when most of the craft shows are held.

○ If you operate a home-maintenance or home-improvement service, you may be busy year-round, but your business is likely to shift indoors and outdoors if you live in a four-season climate. In the fall, for instance, you'll prepare houses for winter; and in the winter, you'll concentrate on indoor projects, such as installing built-in cabinets or painting rooms.

○ If you're an accountant, your busiest time is tax-preparation time, but if you have corporate clients with different fiscal years, you can have several less-hectic busy seasons spread throughout the year.

One Last Test to See If You're Prepared

If you think you're prepared to start freelancing, but you need a little test to make sure, here is one suggestion. Look through local and regional newspapers or through some of your trade magazines for a "start your own business" seminar to attend. If you get bored during the **start-up seminar** because you already know and have already done everything that's discussed, you're prepared. But make sure the seminar is more informational than motivational. You don't need to get caught up in the excitement and let someone talk you into moving before you're ready.

But on the other hand, don't let your own procrastination cause you to let an opportunity slip away.

Deadlines and Dilemmas: Managing the Business Schedule

A freelancer's reputation is his or her business. When the reputation slips, the business slides. So managing your time effectively and productively in order to meet your deadlines is critical. But one reason you became a freelancer is so that you could have some latitude in your work schedule. If you're a morning person, you can start work an hour or two earlier if you want to catch a matinee with a friend or watch a son's afternoon baseball game. But don't start late and take off early, unless you started early and took off late the day before, or you plan to work longer tomorrow...and you actually *do*.

In most cases, before you can manage your time effectively, you have to know how you're spending it. Keeping a log of your activities, noting how long you spend on each one, will give you a starting point for analysis and fine-tuning of your work **schedule.** But if you are in the process of switching from a full-time salaried job to a full-time freelance career, you need a head start on managing your time, so you don't lose too much ground the first week.

As is the case with every other aspect of freelancing, the burden is on you to arrive at a workable schedule.

STARTING A PROJECT PLAN

- Research laws, 3 days
- Apply for Tax I.D. Number
- Organize work space, 5 days
- Have telephone wiring installed
- Convert closet
- Shop for and buy furniture

When beginning a project plan, list all tasks you have to perform. Some tasks are single, self-contained tasks, while others are "subtasks" within a group, or summary task.

In freelancing, you have to keep your overall goals in mind as you complete the daily details. And you have to realize that if you spend too much time on one aspect of a project, then it's going to cost you somewhere else. A good way to keep yourself on schedule is to develop project plans for each assignment. This is especially true if, like most freelancers, you will be working on more than one project at a time. After you have set the plans, draw up a weekly schedule that lays out how you will accomplish your short-term goals.

Develop a Project Plan

A **project plan** is more than a **task list** and schedule. It should include the project's overall **scope,** a list of all tasks that have to be completed and in what sequence, the estimated number of hours needed to complete each task, and the resources required. You can buy computer software from various companies to help you develop project plans, or you can just write it all out on paper.

The advantage of the computer software, however, is its speed and ease in presenting new options when you change a schedule. The software also has built-in prompts that help prevent planning oversights. When you link tasks, a good program will alert you when one task is taking too long for a subsequent task to be started on time. You then have a choice of changing the start date on the second task or adding more resources to the first task, depending on your project's end date. With the computer software, it can take just a few minutes to look at the different options. If you are doing the planning on paper, punching keys on a calculator, and scribbling notes on a calendar, it could take considerably longer—and you're more likely to make a mistake.

Your first project plan could be difficult to develop, but once you get into the routine, the process of planning gets easier. Just take it a step at a time. The example that follows shows how you might plan the process of setting up a home office.

1. Define the scope

This includes a simple statement that summarizes your project, such as "convert the spare bedroom into a home office."

2. Set start and end dates

Give yourself a realistic schedule but do commit to an end date. The project in this example starts on April 1 and ends on April 30, because you start work on a major freelance project on May 1.

3. Develop a task list

Write down all the things that have to be done to have your office ready for operation on April 30. Assign a number to each task, but don't worry too much about putting the tasks in a logical order, you'll do this later. Your list should include everything you can think of, no matter how insignificant it may seem. Examples: 1. Remove bed and store in basement. 2. Remove closet clothes rods. 3. Purchase shelving to convert closet to bookcase. 4. Install shelving in closet. 5. Call telephone company and arrange for telephone voice line and fax line. 6. Develop list of office furniture needed. 7. Develop list of office supplies needed. 8. Develop list of computer, telephone, and related equipment needed. 10. Purchase office furniture. 15. Arrange office furniture...You get the idea. Project plans for truly major assignments will have subtasks and summary tasks.

4. Give each task a timetable

Assign a start and end date for each task, even if these are the same day, and estimate the number of hours it will take to complete the task. Examples: 1. Remove bed and store in basement, April 1–April 1, ½ hour. 2. Remove closet clothes rods, April 1–April 1, ½ hour. 3. Purchase shelving to convert closet to bookcase, April 1–April 1, 2 hours, including travel time to store. 5. Call telephone company and arrange for telephone voice line and fax line, April 1–April 1, ½ to 1 hour, depending on how long you're left on hold by the phone company. There, you've planned half an 8-hour work day already.

5. Establish links between tasks

This just means putting things in order. Although you numbered the tasks 1, 2, 3, etc., this does not establish a sequence, because some tasks may be going on simultaneously, and a high-number task may start one day and continue through several days as low-number tasks are completed. The reason you establish links is to point out potential slips in the schedule that can affect the end date. You cannot install closet shelving before you purchase it, so task 3 has to be a prerequisite for task 4. However, you do not have to perform task 4, installing the shelving, before you take care of task 5, calling the telephone company. Identify the prerequisites for each step. Example: 15. Arrange office furniture, prerequisites: 6, 10, and 12.

It may seem like you're overdoing it, but this exercise will help you plan large projects with complicated steps like these: 82. Deliver revised printout to client for approval, prerequisites: 53 (draft initial report), 61 (get initial report edited), and 75 (design layout and print revised report). Task 53 would have its own prerequisites, also. The links will tell you that to deliver the printout on June 16, you have to complete the draft report by May 15, to allow two weeks for the subcontracted editor to edit it, three days for a manager to review it, one week for the graphic artist to design and lay it out....

6. Assign a resource to each task

This includes both people and materials. Examples: 1. Remove bed..., Larry, Mickey. 2. Remove closet shelves..., Larry. 3. Purchase shelving..., Larry, car.... 5. Call the telephone company..., Larry. This will help you think about what you need besides yourself to get the job done. Hopefully Mickey will be available April 1 to help Larry (the freelancer in this example) move the bed, and hopefully the car is big enough to bring home the shelving. Larry better check on these things. In the example involving the report printout, you would have to make sure the subcontracted editor is available and able to perform the work on schedule.

This exercise will let you know right away if you have overcommitted yourself in terms of time. For instance, if you've assigned three tasks to yourself on the same day, with each task taking 4 hours to complete, you have to plan on working 12 hours that day or rescheduling a task or bringing in an assistant to help you. This is the type of prompt that planning software will give you, if it is programmed to assume an 8-hour workday for each resource person.

7. Update the plan

No plan is totally useful unless you update it regularly. If you're managing a six-month project that involves three or four subcontractors—such as a photographer to shoot product pictures, a writer to create copy, and a printer to print a brochure—then at least a weekly glance at the progress is essential. If the photographer is two days late, how does this affect the printer's schedule? Perhaps the printer only has a window of two or three days in which to print your job before he starts a huge job that will tie up all his equipment. Updating your progress, such as entering a "percent complete" figure each week, will help you to keep your product development on schedule, so you will get your work to the printer on or before your deadline.

A Plan to Manage the Plans

Having a project plan for each assignment helps you schedule the work you do for clients. However, you also have to consider the work you do for yourself. You have to build time into your workday for marketing, purchasing, bookkeeping, all of those things that used to be handled by other people. So, when scheduling tasks for your projects, take time to schedule your personal business as well.

Even though it sounds like you're creating your own little bureaucracy, you need a plan to manage the plans. It can be as elaborate or as basic as you need for your business. Look at it this way: If project A is scheduled from April 15 to September 10, project B from June 14 to August 11, and project C from August 20 to December 15, where does your marketing work fit in so that you can land project D, with work starting December 16? It is easy to put off such things, particularly if marketing and selling are your weak points, but leaving these responsibilities to chance can sooner or later leave you short of cash.

To develop the overall plan and schedule, keep a running list of tasks and responsibilities on a master list that also contains entries from your own business and marketing plans (see Chapters 11 and 13). Again, the master list can be elaborate or basic, whatever fits your needs and prompts you to work on the right thing on the right day. What the master list should tell you most of all is how much of your workday is committed.

Establishing Priorities

Once you have your plans in place, you will see how valuable your time is. You will also see that you have to set **priorities** and make choices about what not to do and who not to see. Many people keep daily task lists handy, and they check off each task as it is completed. This method works if the only thing you have to do is show up for work each day, complete everything you have listed, then go home. If you failed to check off one task, as an employee, you'll probably have a chance to do it tomorrow. But as a freelancer, you have to maintain a broader perspective on your work and time.

You have to complete a certain number of tasks every day. But you also have to look ahead to the next day, week, month, or year to think about what has to be done then, too, to accomplish your overall objectives. And the more tasks you fail to check off one day, the more you have to make up for the next—on your own time. By setting priorities, you can trim the task list to a manageable level and cut out the activities that are either best left to others or best left undone. Revise your list according to your new priorities, and you'll find that you're accomplishing more and feeling less guilty about what you didn't get done. Also, when you're setting priorities, consider both business and personal matters. (See "The Basics of Balancing" in Chapter 7.)

Part of priority setting involves being able to say no. You may have to say no to extra work, to schedule modifications, or to changes in the scope of work. For instance, if you already are overloaded with work, taking on more would result in either lower quality work overall or longer hours that would burn you out. Often, **rush jobs** are not really rush jobs at all, and clients can be persuaded to wait a week. If so, you can fulfill your existing commitments and the new request without overextending yourself or lowering your standards. Of course, there will always be rush jobs, and you will have to take them because they are from regular, good clients. Occasionally, you have to bend your schedule to meet those, but if you can say no to many of the others, you'll have the energy to tackle the really important ones. There also will be rush jobs that you appreciate, such as the ones that fall during a downtime in your schedule.

You may encounter clients at some point that hire you mainly because you are a one-person operation working out of your home, and they look at you as sort of an extended employee whom they can control. You accept a project from them and set up a workable schedule and project plan, then the client comes through with changes in the scope of the product and says, "Oh yeah, I need it a week earlier." To preserve your sanity, self-esteem, and professional image, say no. Usually, the client backs down, and the two of you can work out a solution. If not, then maybe you should put your efforts into finding another client.

Tracking and Analyzing Your Business Time

After you're into freelancing full-time, it is helpful to keep track of what you are doing and how long it takes you to do it. You'll find that this helps you not only in terms of time management, but also in terms of marketing and fee setting (see Chapters 10 and 11). It also helps you to focus on your overall game plan, that is, Am I really doing what I want to do?

Here are some hints to help you track your time effectively:

o Don't lie to yourself. You're not keeping a log that a manager or company president is going to read before deciding on your raise. The log is useful only if it accurately reflects your time.

o Enter time periods in quarter-, half-, or full-hour increments, whatever suits your business best and gives you the best perspective for analysis.

o Enter everything you do during a workday. This includes talking on the telephone—business and personal calls. If a friend drops by for half an hour to show you her new car and take you for a spin, write it down. If the computer breaks down and you spend an hour trying to figure it out yourself before you call the repair service, write that down—especially since it's likely to happen again. If you're lucky enough that it doesn't happen too often, you can call the repair service immediately, then use the downtime to do something fun.

o Keep a running account of your time for at least a representative period. If your project cycle is weekly, keep a log for at least two weeks. But often you can get a clear picture in just a few days.

By the time you finish writing down all those notes on what you were doing and when, you will have a good picture of why . . .

o You're not making any progress on the major project

o You're so tired at 8:00 p.m. every night

o You're never tired and you have so much free time

o You need to be more selective in your choice of computers

o You need to get a voice-mail system to head off calls that simply waste your time

Now comes the analysis. You go back through many of the steps you went through to arrive at your project plans and business plans, and you make adjustments where you think they are necessary. Scheduling for freelancers, as mentioned earlier, is an art form that is usually mastered after a lot of practice and self-analysis. Hopefully, your scheduling abilities will soon focus on the problems of managing a growing work load, rather than on finding enough work to fill up a day. It's just a matter of time.

HOW A WOOD TURNER MIGHT SCHEDULE A QUICK, INTENSIVE JOB

A wood turner needs to produce 60 table legs under a subcontract with a local furniture manufacturer. The table legs are of simple design, and each can be completed in about 30 minutes, plus 10 minutes each setup time. The wood turner accepted the job knowing that the schedule was going to be grueling; he had another project that he had to start no later than one week after he started work on the table legs. The wood turner calculated his production time: 60 table legs X 40 minutes = 2,400 minutes, or 40 hours, enough to fill a normal week's worth of work in production time alone. To meet a quick deadline, get paid quickly, and still meet family obligations, the wood turner drew up his schedule as follows:

Friday:	Sign contract with furniture manufacturer, get wood delivered to shop.
Saturday:	8:00–10:00, get shop organized, wood in place, pattern analyzed, trial run made, and anticipated problems solved. 10:30–12:00, mow the lawn. 2:00–4:30, attend local school fair with family.
Sunday:	Long-planned day trip with family.
Monday:	7:00–11:30, turning session. 12:00–1:30, lunch at the civic club meeting. 2:00–5:30, turning session. 7:30–9:00, additional turning session. Day's results: 9.5 hours production, 14 table legs.
Tuesday:	7:00–12:00, turning session. 1:30–5:30, turning session. 7:00–9:00, additional turning session. Day's results: 11 hours turning, 16 table legs, 30 total.
Wednesday:	7:00–12:00, turning session. 1:00–1:30, meeting with other client on next week's project. 2:00–6:00, turning session. 7:30, family dinner for a relative's birthday. Day's results: 9 hours production, 13 table legs, 43 total.
Thursday:	7:00–12:00, turning session. 1:00–5:00, turning session. Day's results: 9 hours production, 13 table legs, 56 total, 93 percent of project completed.
Friday:	7:00-12:00, turning session completes production of 60th table leg, inspection of the products, re-turning of defective pieces. 2:00–3:00, deliver products to client. 4:00–5:30, set up for next week's project.

PART FOUR

WHERE DO YOU FREELANCE?

CHAPTER SEVEN

Teenage Daughters Don't Always Understand

KEY TERMS

balance

mental space

philosophical questions

focus

perspective

work space

If you're a married freelancer, particularly one with children, deciding where to set up your office is a family decision. *And you thought you were going to be your own boss.* The first two considerations are an office and a telephone. A separate room with a tightly closing door is best for an office, especially if it's away from the main household traffic. It's also best to be away from the kitchen, which tends to be the busiest—and noisiest—room in the house. Get your own telephone line installed in the office. It drives teenage daughters nuts—not to mention the fact that it's really unfair—when they can't use the telephone after school. You may have to

hold a family meeting periodically to keep the household and business running smoothly.

If you're single, though, you probably have a few more options, but you still have quite a few decisions to make. Your office setup will depend on the size of your residence. If you live in a loft apartment in midtown Manhattan or a studio apartment in an Atlanta high-rise, you probably don't have much choice about where you put your office. But if you own a sprawling ranch house in Texas or a cabin with a detached garage in rural Oregon, you'll have plenty of options. Whatever your situation, you'll have to decide whether freelancing is your whole life, consuming a major portion of your living environment, or just your business life, limited to specific physical areas.

Setting up and managing a business in the home involves solving both practical and personal issues. Chapter 8 deals with the practicalities of designing and equipping the home office. But before you get down to the physical work of installing a fax machine and converting closets to bookcases, it's a good idea to get your mind in tune with the realities of working at home.

Deciding how much space you need involves more than just measuring off a section of the basement and drawing a chalk layout of where you want things to go. It also involves assessing how much **mental space** the business will occupy in you and anyone else who lives in the house with you. If you've worked away from home for 10 years, and your family isn't used to having you around the house all the time, your presence will change the amount of mental space you occupy in their lives.

For instance, if your business requires you to use your kitchen for baking or cooking, such as in a home-based catering business, where do the kids fit in when they come home from school? You've just invaded their sacred routine of guiltlessly scavenging food from all corners of the kitchen. If your business involves using the residential telephone line at least part of the time, then who answers the telephone after school and how do they answer it? A client won't like the prospect of talking to a child, and the child won't like the prospect of talking to an adult. Even when you work

at home, you need some separation of work and home—physically and mentally.

You can attain this separation best by keeping a steady **balance** in your business and personal affairs. Deciding up front where you want to work and how it fits in with the scheme of things at home is important. But there undoubtedly will be points you overlook until you actually start working at home.

Maintaining a Balance In Your Business And Personal Lives

When you're a freelancer, you have to work hard and work long hours, because you are performing both the work and some or all of the support services, such as marketing, bookkeeping, filing, and office cleaning. In the meantime, if you're married with children, you have to pay attention to being a spouse and a parent. And if you're single, you still need some sort of social life to keep from burning yourself out the first six months you're in business.

One way to look at this balancing dilemma is to compare it to a photographer sizing up a scene through a 35mm camera. To get a variety of shots from the same position, the photographer would need a 28mm wide-angle lens, a 50mm normal lens, and a 80–210mm telephoto zoom lens. He or she would use the wide-angle lens to get the big picture. This would compare to your overall goals. To focus on the normal view, the view the human eye sees, the photographer would use a 50mm lens. This would compare to your day-to-day tasks and responsibilities. The zoom lens would be the fun part. The photographer could put it up to 210mm and focus on a distant point—perhaps a goal you want to reach. Then gradually, he or she could pull the zoom back to 80mm, stopping at various points to size up the composition. You could consider these intermediate stops as steps you have to conquer along the way to that distant goal.

The camera analogy is just a way to introduce an idea that is critical to balancing your work and life: **focus.** And just as professional photographers are constantly focusing and refocusing their lenses as they work, so too will you be focusing and refocusing your efforts throughout the course of your freelancing career. Goals change and so do methods of achieving them. You have to develop your own method of keeping yourself focused—on what you want to do, for whom, how and why you want to do it, and how you want to be rewarded for it. And where you work is a critical factor in this equation.

A fast way to lose your footing as a freelancer is to get lost in doing everything everybody else wants you to do. You lose professionally, because you can't focus your work performance on such a wide-angle field. And you lose personally, because you won't be able to provide for or spend enough time with your family. By focusing properly, you can define your freelancing goals and methods, identify your preferred market, develop a satisfactory compensation structure, and meet your personal goals as well.

An easy temptation when you work at home is tending to too many home chores at times when you should be working. That's just the opposite of when you worked overtime at the office and neglected taking care of things around the house. But at least when you worked at the corporate office, you got a paycheck. If you don't work at home, you don't get paid. How you set up your home office physically can help in easing these temptations, but it's just as much a mental consideration as a physical one. In other words, you have to stay focused and balanced.

The Basics of Balancing

One way to gain a foothold on balance before freelancing knocks you down is to step back and make a few not-so-simple decisions.

You can do this before you go into full-time freelancing, and you can do it periodically after you've become a freelancer, as a way of assessing your business and personal goals and achievements.

Ask yourself some **philosophical questions** to help create your big picture. Each of your answers has an effect on your overall plan. If you break your answers down into business and personal components, you will start to get a sharper focus on how to balance your life.

Following is a list of basic questions to ask yourself and some examples of possible answers.

What Do I Want to Be?

Professionally:
Respected in my field, financially successful.
Personally:
A good spouse, a good parent, comfortable with myself.

To Whom Do I Want to Be It?

Professionally:
To the public, to other businesses, to a limited number of clients, to anyone who will pay the bills.
Personally:
To myself, to my spouse, to my children, to my parents, to my friends, to Uncle Bill (or any other mentor or special person).

When Do I Want to Do It?

Professionally:
9:00 A.M. to 5:00 P.M.; 4:00 A.M. to 2:00 P.M.; whatever it takes; five, six, or seven days a week.
Personally:
Until the kids are finished with high school, forever, until the economy improves to the point that I can work in a regular job with great benefits again.

How Do I Want to Do It?

Professionally:
In small doses in the beginning, then full speed ahead; by taking only enough money out of the business to exist and putting everything else back in to build up the business; by improving my marketing and selling skills to keep cash flowing.
Personally:
By continually considering the business and personal consequences of major decisions; by scheduling my work around the family's important occasions and events, working harder some days to allow time off on other days.

Where Do I Want to Do It?

Professionally:
In the spare bedroom, in the basement, in the garage, all over the house.
Personally:
In the town where I grew up and have lived all my life; where we live now, then when the kids get out of school, in a town with a warmer climate and a more stable economy.

What Am I Willing to Give Up To Make a Success of It?

Professionally:
The camaraderie of office coworkers, the convenience of having others do my selling and bookkeeping for me, the ability to use a corporation's computer equipment and copy machine.
Personally:
The security of a regular paycheck and more health insurance, hours of recreation time to make up for extra work loads, the view from an office tower.

How Do I Want to Be Rewarded?

Professionally:

Make lots of money, make enough money to be financially secure after sending kids to college, be known as a respected resource person in my field, have the satisfaction of knowing I performed well and to the satisfaction of my clients or customers.

Personally:

Build equity in a business to sell when I retire, just have a profession I can practice until I retire, have a life where I can both work successfully and enjoy life as an individual and as a family member.

Why Do I Want to Do It?

Professionally:

To be my own boss, to try new methods, to make a mark in my profession.

Personally:

To be able to see my kids grow up on a daily basis rather than just at night and on weekends, to feel secure within myself, to not have to rely on other people to provide me with an income, to spend more time with my family.

At Home, Advantages And Disadvantages Are Often the Same

As you develop your philosophical approach by answering the previous questions, you may want to consider some of the basic advantages and disadvantages of working at home. In many ways an advantage is also a disadvantage, depending on how you manage yourself and where you work within your home.

You can turn commuting time into work time and get more done. That is an advantage in working at home. But how much of your other time will you also turn into work time? A common problem for home-based freelancers is the tendency to overwork. Your office is in the house. You don't have to drive 30 minutes or take a 45-minute train ride to get there. You might as well be working, so you can make more money, you rationalize. Writers, especially, tend to think this way. They get an idea and want to see how it looks on the computer screen. It's not the same as scribbling on a notepad and dealing with it tomorrow "at the office." But in many cases, that's exactly what you should do.

A common freelancer ailment, especially when you are on a tight deadline, is feeling like you have to get right into your home office and get to work as soon as you get out of bed in the morning. Just get that cup of coffee and sit down at the computer. Sometimes, you don't even want to take a shower first. Who's going to smell you anyway?

There is an easy solution to this, however. Get up a few minutes earlier, sit down in a comfortable chair, and sip your coffee and nibble a bagel while you read the newspaper. This will remind you that there is a world outside, and that will help you keep your **perspective.** Besides, having breakfast this way is better for you than gulping it down in front of the computer.

One solution to the "I feel guilty when I'm not working" problem is to develop a consistent work schedule with which you and your family are comfortable. Also, set up your work area in such a way that, for the most part, when you're home, you're not at work and when you're at work, you're not at home. One reason you're freelancing is to blend home and work more than you have in the past, but you also have to have enough balance to keep your personal and business lives separate.

In most books about home-based working, you'll see listed as an advantage saving money on restaurant or take-out lunches. This can also be a disadvantage, not so much financially as personally. With a kitchen full of food just feet from your office or shop, will you be able to resist having too many snacks during the workday? Will you eat too many meals at your desk or work bench and not get the best benefits from the food?

One solution is to schedule lunch just like you would if you worked outside the home. Perhaps you can time it so that you can have a sandwich while watching the noon news on television. It's just as important to take a lunch break when you work at home as it is when you work away from home. Where you eat can make a difference in your perspective on the day. A few minutes away from the shop or office can help you get a better view of the problem you wrestled with all morning. A break can help you see things from a new perspective—something coworkers did previously.

Speaking of coworkers, how will the family pets take your working at home? With the family dog at your heels all day, and no other person in sight, will you start bouncing ideas off Dee Dee the

Pekinese and expect her to give you the right answers? Or will you take her for a walk every time you encounter a slow moment in work, thereby wasting 20 minutes—10 of which you spend telling the dog to "pee!" when she really doesn't have to—instead of spending only 5 minutes to get a drink of water or another cup of coffee before getting back to work?

Will you be able to continue working when Casper the white cat crawls up into your lap and starts purring? Or will you have to shut off your work area to your pets at times? Incidentally, it is best to keep cat hair out of your computer equipment, which means that even if it's a warm spot, the laser printer is not a cat bed. This may sound trivial now, but it won't be when you're printing out a report—and invoice—on deadline, and the printer jams because of the cat.

Another pet issue is noise. If you spend a great deal of time on the phone in your work, a dog barking or a bird chirping in the background can be distracting, and others will consider it unprofessional. You may be so used to the bird chirping that you don't even hear it—until a client asks you what the heck is all that noise in the background. Granted, a bird chirping in your office is more pleasant than a siren wailing outside your former city office, but clients don't think twice about sirens.

Family, Friends, And Business

Once you've achieved a separation between your work and home life, you

---

A FREELANCING PARENT'S PLIGHT

Advantage: **Working at home gives a freelancer the opportunity to be readily available to his or her children.**

Disadvantage: **Working at home gives a freelancer the opportunity to be readily available to his or her children.**

I received a call the other day from my teenage daughter. Could I come and pick her and Jen up from school? This was not the first time in recent weeks that I'd received this call and—with a pattern of me as her regular chauffeur forming—I asked her, "Why don't you ever call Jen's mother?"

"Because she works!" I was told.

To many kids, anything a parent does in the home is not work. "To work" is a place parents go each day, in another building, somewhere else. To convince your children that you are indeed working in that spare room may be one of the most difficult assignments for a freelancer.

For spouses and parents, the decision to freelance out of your home is a family decision. Children who are old enough to understand the concept of "going to work" need to be included up front in the decision.

— Margaret Heinrich Hand
Full-Time Freelance Writer/Editor

have to make sure your family and friends respect it. The box "A Freelancing Parent's Plight" illustrates a common problem.

A perception that some people, especially relatives and family members, have is that if you're home, it's OK to call you anytime. They don't have to tell a "nosy" secretary who's calling before they get you on the phone. You will get called about anything and everything until these people realize that you are working at home, just like you were working at the other place.

If this is a big problem that causes you to lose valuable work time, then one solution is to put on the voice-mail system or the answering machine, something that lets you monitor your calls. You also may want to get a call-waiting feature on your telephone, so you don't miss an important business call when a relative is on the line, or vice versa.

If you have children and they are one of the main reasons you want to work at home, you'll likely find they also can be one of the main distractions to your work. The degree of potential problems depends on the ages of the children.

If they are older children who are used to having the run of the house for a few hours after school, they'll have to adjust to coming home and finding you there every day. In most cases, you can talk things out in advance, but it won't be until you are actually working at home that the children fully realize their daily routines have changed. Their feelings can, and probably will, range from extreme happiness at having you there to great disappointment at having lost their daytime privacy. Solutions vary from household to household but can range from reworking your schedule to be available to them most or part of the time, to sealing off your work area to the point that they really have to look for you to know you're there.

Younger children require more time and will need a greater degree of consideration when you set up your home office. You may need to schedule work only during certain hours. Or you may have to consider sending your child to day care even though you work at home. Day care is often the only solution to having the right kind of time to perform your work professionally. Fortunately, the proper day-care environment can help your child develop his or her own social skills, so the time away can be good for both of you. If you cannot afford a day-care center or are adamantly opposed to the idea, see if you can hire a baby-sitter or nanny to come into the house and help.

Just when you thought you had it all worked out, with the kids involved in wholesome after-school activities and

You don't have to put a sign on your home-office door like the one above, but you do have to reach an understanding with everyone who lives with you regarding your work area, schedule, and general business arrangements.

you getting your work done on time, it hits you. School's out! It's summer! All of a sudden, you have a big project due by July 15, and your home has been invaded by screaming, running, jumping little people. Summer presents a special problem for home-based freelancers who are parents of school-age children.

Again, the range of problems and solutions depends on the ages of the children. Part of the summer can be consumed by sending the kids to camp, an option you probably would have chosen even if you weren't working at home. Older children may have a summer job. Then again, you may be able to employ your own children to do certain tasks, either in your business or in the home. Make a list of the options and talk them over with your family before summer hits, so the transition will go smoother.

Defining Your Work Space

You need to define your **work space** by considering all the above factors, plus other needs, including whether you need to have a separate outside entrance for visiting clients to use and whether you need to baby-proof your work area for a small child.

One way to see if this home-office situation is going to work is to make a list of what the office needs to satisfy everyone, including the clients, kids, and pets. Then, since you can never satisfy everyone, pare the list down according to your established priorities and what you can afford. If it takes a $35,000 addition to your house to satisfy only one or two requirements, they may not be worth it. If those requirements relate to your family's needs, call a meeting and decide if you can all live within the existing space until the business grows.

If the requirements relate to business needs, such as a separate entrance for clients, reassess why you listed that requirement. Maybe there's a way for you to go to your clients' offices instead of having them come to you. Also, try and determine how much business you may lose by not having the separate entrance, then see if there is a way to make up the lost business with other types of business.

Setting up and maintaining a home office is not as simple as it seems, but if you work through the right processes when making decisions, it's a manageable feat—something millions of people do every day.

CHAPTER EIGHT

The Freelancer's Workplace

KEY TERMS

computer   fax machine

inventory   organization

software   wish list

After deciding to work at home, and choosing the general area in which you want to do it, you have to organize physically. You need a comfortable space and, if you expect to have clients visit you in your home office, a professional environment. You may work best on a messy desk, but you need to have that desk in a workable place, and it can't be so messy that you can't quickly clean it up before a client arrives.

Some considerations:

o A woodworker's bench needs to be in a position that is safe and accessible.

o A photographer's lab needs to be workable and environmentally safe.

o The telephone has to be within easy reach so you don't lose an important call.

But after making all the philosophical and personal decisions related to establishing and running a home-based free-lancing business, actually creating your own work environment can be fun and exciting. The objective is to fill a physical space with the tools you need, on a budget you can afford, and to arrange these tools for optimum performance and for a professional image. Even if you don't receive clients or customers at home, a professional image in your own mind helps to promote a professional attitude.

Developing a budget for your home-office setup involves making a **wish list,** trimming it to suit your finances, and adjusting it to fit your space and design plans. You can do this in three phases. First, take stock of what you have and list what you think you need in terms of tools, furniture, office equipment and supplies, and business stationery. Next, analyze where you will be working to see how all of the items on your wish list will fit. Then, design and fill your work environment. You may want to develop two or three different projected budgets, from "bare minimum" to "good working conditions" to "absolute tops."

Take Inventory and Make a Wish List

If you've been practicing your free-lancing profession as someone else's employee, or as a serious hobbyist or part-timer while working in an unrelated occupation, then you may already have many of the things you consider tools of the trade. For writers, this includes a computer and printer; for woodworkers, a basic collection of woodworking tools and machines; for photographers, two or three cameras and possibly a dark-room; for computer consultants, a computer and a variety of utilities and peripherals; and for potters, a potter's wheel and a kiln.

A good place to start in outfitting your home working environment is to take **inventory** of your existing tools. As part of that inventory, write down the quality level of your tools. Are they professional or amateur models? Will they survive the daily grind as well as they have under occasional use? Are they reliable enough for you to depend on them for heavy-duty use? If not, how long will you be able to use them before you have to replace them?

Then, make another list, one that contains everything you think you'll need to perform your work professionally. Again, write down the quality level for the desired tools. You may want some to be industrial-strength; for others, quality may be less important, because you will only use them occasionally, even after you're a full-time freelancer. Through mail-order catalogs, newspaper ads, or phone calls and store visits, determine the cost of the new tools.

Look around and see what office furniture you already have. Evaluate—using the same professional/amateur system you used with your tools—whether you can use this furniture in your business. Now, list what furniture you will need to buy. Search through the telephone book, mail-order catalogs, and office super-store catalogs to get ideas and price ranges. Points to keep in mind are comfort and workability. If you are going to be working at a computer most of the day, you need a good, comfortable chair and a desk that is the correct ergonomic configuration. Typical office furniture includes a desk or table, a chair, a filing cabinet, and a lamp.

One consideration when choosing furniture is whether you need a particular type of desk or shelving. You may be able to barter for what you need. For instance, a local furniture refinisher may have a recently restored desk and book-case unit that is perfect for your office,

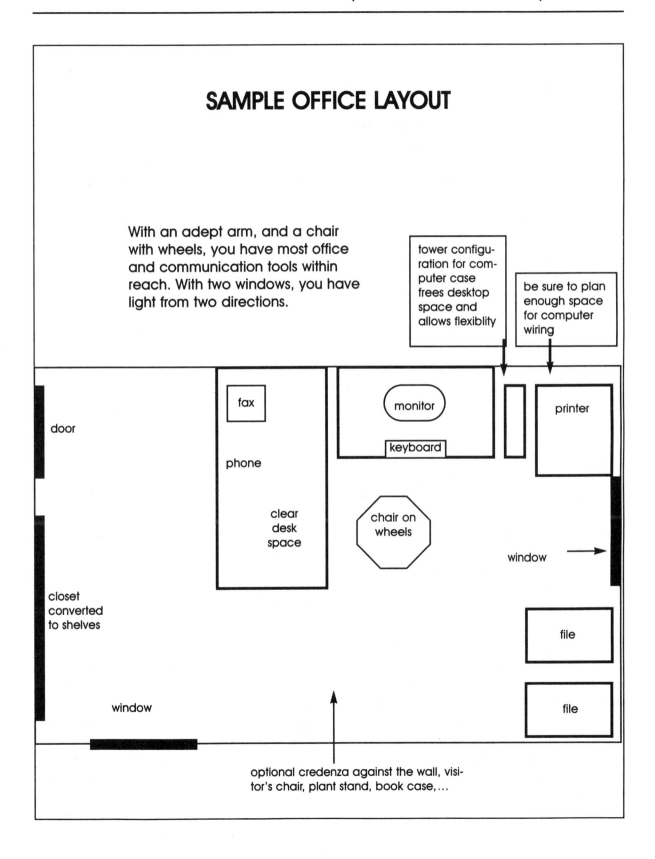

SAMPLE OFFICE LAYOUT

With an adept arm, and a chair with wheels, you have most office and communication tools within reach. With two windows, you have light from two directions.

tower configuration for computer case frees desktop space and allows flexiblity

be sure to plan enough space for computer wiring

door

fax

phone

clear desk space

monitor

keyboard

printer

chair on wheels

window

closet converted to shelves

file

file

window

optional credenza against the wall, visitor's chair, plant stand, book case,...

and he may be willing to trade you for your expertise in advertising. Just keep accurate records of the barter, so you can explain it to your accountant, since you may be liable for taxes on the trade.

Beyond furniture, the amount and types of office equipment you'll need depends on what business you're in. But, as in furniture, there are some basics. The first things you will need will be a telephone and an answering device for your business phone line. If you already have these, good. Just make sure the hardware is working properly, that you can hear well through it, and that your clients can hear you well. Your answering device can be a $39 answering machine or a sophisticated voice-mail system that you have custom-designed for your needs. You can even run the voice mail through your computer.

You'll also need a **fax machine** if you plan to do much communicating with other business people. This has become the standard mode of operation for many companies when they order products by telephone, confirm appointments, or send out queries regarding services and products. It also has become a standard method of invoicing for services and products.

Fax machines come in a variety of qualities, offering a full range of capabilities. You can get by with a $300 basic machine, or you can get a much more expensive one if you want it to print on plain paper as opposed to thermal paper. A fax machine can double as a limited copier. You can only copy single sheets of paper that fit through the fax machine and not bound books or magazines.

An alternative to the fax machine is a fax/modem built into your computer system. This way, you don't have to print every fax you receive before reading it. But you do have to take time to sort through the software that comes with the fax/modem, time that sometimes is better spent elsewhere. Whether you should use a fax/modem or not depends on the capacity of your computer and how it figures into your specific business. Sometimes, it's just simpler to have a machine for each purpose, a computer for a computer and a fax machine for a fax machine.

The **computer** is a major piece of office equipment. While not essential to some freelancers, it is nevertheless becoming a standard desktop—or laptop—fixture in the home and in home-based businesses. Computers are the focus of many businesses, and deciding which computer to buy is a time-consuming, often frustrating experience. Sometimes, the more you know about computers, the more frustrating it is, because the market is extremely volatile and price sensitive.

How to Buy a Computer System

When you ask a computer consultant which computer you should buy, you're likely to be answered with the question, "What do you want to do with it?" When you ask a computer salesperson which kind of computer you should buy, you're likely to get a different question, "How much can you spend?" Both questions are appropriate responses.

But you, as the computer user, will have to decide for yourself how the two issues come together.

First, you have to realize that the moment you buy your computer, it—like a new car—is worth less than you paid for it. Technology is advancing so fast that six months down the road you'll be able to buy a better computer for less money. So the first recommendation is to buy what you need that is within your budget, and don't think too much about future price trends.

Deciding whether to buy a "PC" or a "Mac" is the first decision to make. PCs are IBM-compatible machines. Macs are Macintosh machines made by Apple Computer. The two have different operating systems, and people usually have a definite preference as to which one they want to use. Or they already know how to use one of the systems because of previous work experience. While the Macs have long been graphically oriented and are generally considered to be easier to use, running Microsoft Windows–based programs on PCs can make them graphically oriented also. The best way to choose a system is to test them at a computer dealer that sells both.

Besides personal preference, you may want to consider what systems are used by companies with whom you may be exchanging electronic files. While you can use translation programs to read and write documents across the two platforms, it's an extra step that consumes time and sometimes is unreliable. If, for instance, you're a writer who will be sending numerous disks to publishers, you have to make sure the publishers can read your disks on their equipment. If the overwhelming number of publishers have PCs, then you should give this some consideration. But if you're in desktop publishing or in design and drafting, the trend is likely to be toward the Mac.

Regardless of which operating system you choose, make sure you have enough power to do what you want to do. This is where the computer consultant's question comes in. If all you want to do is run basic word-processing and simple bookkeeping programs, you can get by with pretty much any off-the-shelf system. But if your requirements are greater, get a system with a huge hard drive, a CD-ROM drive, and at least 8 megabytes (8 MB) of random access memory (RAM). The amount of RAM helps to control how fast your computer will let you work. The more complex the software, the more RAM you need. While 4 MB has been the standard RAM for a few years, 8 MB has been increasingly necessary for many programs.

The type of processor your computer uses also affects the work speed. In the Macs, processors go by such names as 68030 or 68040, with the higher number indicating greater speed. In PCs, processors can be one of the 486 options or one of the newest Intel Pentiums. The 486 processor comes in SX and DX versions, with DX meaning that a math coprocessor speeds up complex calculations, a nice feature if you're run-

---

OFFICE FURNITURE AND EQUIPMENT TIPS:

o If you have a tight budget and can only get one really good piece of furniture, put your money where you sit. A good, comfortable chair can get you through the day without adding to your fatigue. A cheap, bad chair can make you too uncomfortable to work.

o If you need to save money and you have some time, ready-to-assemble (RTA) furniture can be less expensive. There is a wide range of RTA furniture available, so just make sure you get what you need. Otherwise, you'll be replacing it in a few weeks or months.

o The more you expect your fax machine to do, the more you can expect something to go wrong. Some fax machines can double as regular telephones, and some even have built-in answering machines. But if the answering machine breaks down, you also lose your fax machine. Usually, separate pieces of equipment work better.

o If your office is narrow and has little room in the center, perhaps lateral files would be better than conventional filing cabinets. You can see more files, and the unit requires less pull-out space.

o Paper trays are excellent office accessories to help you organize your paperwork, as long as you use them the proper way. Stuffing them with mail you don't know what to do with is not the proper use. To get better organized you can start with basic "In" and "Out" trays. From there, you can have trays for various levels of action, such as "Do This Today," "Pending Return Mail/Fax," or "End-of-Month Duties."

---

ning a graphics program, a design or drafting program, or an intensive accounting or spreadsheet package. Also, among the newer offerings are processors that run both Mac and IBM programs.

A wide range of qualities exists in computer monitors. If you are going to be staring at a computer screen all day, you'll want to invest in the best possible monitor, such as one with a good rating. For example, in IBM-compatibles, the lower the number in dot-pitch ratings, the better. A .28 dot-pitch monitor is better than a .54 dot-pitch, for example.

Again, the basic goal here is to get the most powerful computer system you can afford now. Prices tend to drop at the end of the calendar year, but you can find sales all year long in this highly competitive market. Count on replacing or upgrading your computer, however, in three to four years.

Don't Forget the Peripherals

In addition to the computer and monitor, you will want to get some peripheral pieces for certain functions, including a modem or fax/modem and a printer. The modem often is bundled with different computer systems anyway, but if it isn't, try and get at least one that rates at 14,400 bps (bits per second) for data transfer. The modem is essential if you subscribe to one of the on-line computer services or if you plan to use the Internet.

Printers you buy according to budget and intended use.

o *Dot-matrix printers* were the workhorses of computer printing for many years. They still are viable printers for certain purposes, such as printing wide ledger sheets and multipart accounting forms and printing fast draft copies of reports. Even a color dot-matrix printer is not that expensive any more. But be warned, dot-matrix printers are very noisy. Price range: $100–$300.

o *Ink-jet printers* are the next step up. Their print quality is better than dot-matrix, and you can use them for printing professional-looking letters and correspondence. However, the cost for their use, in terms of ink cartridges, etc., can be expensive if you have a tendency to print out everything, every step of the way. These printers offer color printing at entry-level costs, but the colors are limited

in terms of quality. Price range: $275–$600, depending on brand and whether you get color.

o *Laser printers* are increasing in popularity as their prices become more competitive. You need a laser printer if you're in desktop publishing, but for other occupations, your needs are set by the quality of printing you want to do and the speed at which you want to do it. Laser printers are the best choice for the combination of quality and speed, but if you're looking for color, plan on spending thousands if you want laser color. Price range: $500 and up.

Finally, there are a few computer accessories that most serious computer users consider necessary. One is a surge suppressor, which prevents power surges from destroying the computer. That runs $6 and up, depending on brand and quality. You may opt for an uninterrupted power supply, which can combine surge suppression with the capacity to keep your computer on and operating for a short period after the power goes out, allowing you time to save whatever you are working on and exit gracefully. The power units sell for about $120 and up.

Some type of backup system is necessary if you depend on the computer for your livelihood. A variety of tape drives are available, beginning at about $150. You use the tape backup to store anything that's important, possibly the entire contents of your hard drive. This way, if your hard drive ever fails, you'll be able to restore the data to a recovered or new hard drive.

Choose Software That Fits Your Needs

Computer **software** comes in the full range of prices and complexity. Software you choose according to how you plan to use it and how important the computer is to your business. If the computer is just a tool to write letters, track customer accounts, and do simple bookkeeping, then you don't need a lot of complicated software. But if your occupation is computer intensive, the software you need can get both complicated and expensive, as you probably already know.

The simpler programs cost less than $100 each, often less than $50. In this price range, you can get a financial program to keep the books and maybe print checks using the computer, or you can get a simple word-processing package to write letters and fill out invoices.

For around $100, you can get what's known as an integrated software package. These packages, which typically are quite good for the occasional or light-business computer user, usually have the word *works* in their name. They have word-processing, database, spreadsheet, and sometimes accessory programs built into one package. The word processor is usually more advanced than ones found in the individual lower-priced programs. The database function gives you the ability to track customers, trends, or reference information quickly and smoothly.

And the spreadsheet program gives you a way to keep track of your finances.

Beyond the integrated programs, you can buy individual higher-powered software programs in the $300 price range, or you can buy into one of the "suite" offerings. The suites bundle three or more of the more powerful programs into one package and sell in the $450–$500 price range. They offer a cost-effective way to buy software, because you can usually get three or more programs for less than the price of two. In the suites, you can get word-processing, spreadsheet, and presentation software. Some also offer database programs.

Now, Gather Up Your Belongings...

Organization leads to efficiency in freelancing. And, assuming you are competent and professional in your chosen occupation, efficiency leads to profits. The home office is where it all starts.

Once you know what items you need or can afford, take a look at your available space. On a piece of paper draw an outline of the work area, including dimensions, peculiar characteristics, and limitations. If you're a craft artisan, you may have to work around the only corner where you can install the proper ventilation system. Or, perhaps, the only way you can arrange the area so that you have your own business entrance is to place your desk to the right of the office's only window. Or you may find that a cubbyhole is the perfect size for your computer table. You can draw a basic outline of your office, then make copies to use to develop several alternatives.

Use your space to the maximum benefit. This means putting in only the furniture and equipment you need and arranging it in the most efficient way. The question to ask when deciding whether to keep an item in your work area is, "What business purpose does this serve?" If you can't think of any, put the item in the already overcrowded basement or get rid of it.

If you are a woodworker or a blacksmith, then you can organize your work area according to your normal work flow. You need your tools set up so that when you finish one task, you can easily move to the next one. Think of yourself as an efficient one-person assembly line. If you're a writer, you need a computer setup that is comfortable and ergonomically safe, plus you need a desk area that is uncluttered enough for you to spread out reference books without having to swipe away a bunch of other stuff first. If you're a management consultant, you need a lot of things at your fingertips—computer, telephone, directories, source books, and fax machine.

Turning a spare bedroom into an office often gives you the advantage of converting a clothes closet into a shelving system. By installing adjustable shelf brackets, you can adapt the closet to your changing needs. You can use some shelves as a bookcase and others as an open filing system for a long-term project. If the closet has bi-fold doors, opening them in the morning and closing them when you quit for the day helps to give you a sense of coming to and leaving from work—a small point, but when you're a lonely freelancer, every little thing helps. You may even want to hide the computer in the closet, keeping it out of sight unless you're using it.

Customizing the Work Space

In most cases, you'll be converting some type of room or a section of the garage, basement, or attic into a work area. In doing this, consider comfort and workability. If you will have clients visiting you in your work area, then you also need to make image a consideration. But also, keep in mind long-range possibilities and the potential for growth. It's usually more cost effective to plan in advance.

For instance:

o When you have the phone line installed, arrange for the capability to add an additional line or two in the future. You may only want one line right now, which you will use for both voice and fax calls, but later you may want separate lines for the fax and computer and an additional voice line.

o When installing electrical wiring, make sure you have adequate capacity, plus expansion capability, for all tools you use or plan to use. Also, if the room does not have central air conditioning, make sure you can plug in a window unit in the summertime. Not losing two or three days of effective work will more than offset the cost of a small window air conditioner. Also, if the room is cold in the wintertime, make sure you can plug in a portable heater at a convenient and safe spot.

o If you deal at all with chemicals or if your operation produces any kind of dust, make sure your ventilation system is not only adequate and legal for now, but that it is expandable. You may need outside, specialized help with this.

o Consider colors and how they affect you. Does a beige wall bore you, or do you have no feelings either way? Would you work better if the wall had cheery, bright wallpaper? Is the floor covering unappealing? Would a black-and-white tile floor look more professional? Make your choices based on personal preferences and professional considerations.

o Installing fluorescent lighting fixtures can lower your electric bill over the long term. If you don't like the effect of a cool white fluorescent bulb, try using a warm or deluxe warm white fluorescent bulb.

o If you are a heavy computer user, you might consider having an electrician run a wire just for your computer equipment. Have the wire connected to its own circuit breaker to relieve the pressure on other household functions and vice versa.

o Consider noise factors. Does your business make a lot of noise? If so, extra soundproofing could be needed. On the other hand, if your office is in a room that looks out over a school playground, you'll need a way to block the noise at recess.

Keep Up with the Times

Technology has enabled millions of people to work at home. To continue working at home, you need to stay apace with the changing technology related to your profession and to business in general. Maybe you don't need a computer today, but you need to keep an open mind about getting one if it helps you in business. Maybe you don't need a fax machine today. But if you land an account that requires one, you need to be able to go out and make an intelligent purchase.

Staying abreast of trends in home-office furnishings and equipment is especially helpful if you outfitted your first home office with items from the rest of the house. Switching from an old table and chair to an ergonomically superior workstation may be just what you need to give yourself an efficiency boost in your second year of operation. If you've kept up with prices and styles, you'll be better able to make a quick decision when the time comes to buy the workstation.

PART FIVE

HOW DO YOU FREELANCE?

CHAPTER NINE

Legalities and Technicalities

KEY TERMS

contract

partnership

tax identification number

corporation

sole proprietorship

zoning

It is always best to determine all legal requirements for your business up front. Determining whether your operation is legal is like playing 20 questions, then calling the lawyer to see if the answers will get you a fine, jail time, or your children sued by a distant relative. Pesky as they are, legalities and technicalities are not trivialities when it comes to going into—and staying in—business. And usually, they're not funny either.

Answer the following questions with "yes;" "no;" "what do you mean?;" or "I don't think that applies to me." The longer your answers, the more you need professional advice.

○ Do I need a business license?

○ Have I filed a fictitious-name statement?

○ Do I have a standard contract for people to sign when they engage my services?

○ Have I drawn up a will and specified what is to happen to my business, business property, and business liabilities if I die unexpectedly?

○ Does my homeowner's liability insurance extend to my business?

○ Does my home office conform to the local zoning ordinances?

o Have I filed the proper registration forms with state and federal tax agencies regarding my proprietorship, partnership, or corporation?

o Do I have a federal tax identification number?

o Do I have to collect and pay sales taxes?

When in Doubt, Seek Help

Many of the tasks associated with the legal aspects of freelancing can be performed by anyone with a knack for research and the tenacity to fill out an endless array of forms. But even if you have the ability to write your own incorporation papers, it is still a good idea to get a lawyer to review them before you send them to the secretary of state. There may be one or two points you should make clear—or vague—enough to protect yourself. For instance, you don't want to limit the scope of your corporation so much that you cannot expand later on.

It's best to set aside a chunk of money in the beginning that you resign yourself to spending on a lawyer and an accountant. How big a chunk depends on how much of the legwork you're willing to do yourself and, of course, how plush the furnishings are in your lawyer's and accountant's offices. Ask around and you might find professionals working out of their homes, too, who are willing to answer the bunch of questions you've researched yourself.

You can use an accountant or lawyer for a range of services, from a $100 business setup counseling session to a full-blown they-do-the-work-you-sign-the-papers deal. With most freelancers, the answer is somewhere between these extremes. The tricky part is knowing when to call your lawyer—*before* you get into trouble—and when not to call her, because you can figure it out yourself at a lower hourly rate. As for the accountant, knowing when to hand over your tax paperwork is something you and he will have to work out.

The basic business setup counseling session may be all you need. If you have more time than money, you can do all the business research yourself, including tending to the points mentioned in this chapter. Once you have everything together, you can discuss the legal and tax aspects with a lawyer, an accountant, or both. They can then tell you what you missed, how you should follow up, how to set up your accounting records, what clauses to insert into every contract, and whether you should remain a proprietorship instead of becoming a corporation.

One advantage in doing all the legwork yourself is you get to know what local and state officials are responsible for various processes. When you have questions after you're in business, you can call them instead of a lawyer.

But if you don't have a lot of time, and you can budget a few hundred dollars toward the legal and accounting setup costs, by all means, let the professionals do the work. It can make your life a lot easier.

Assuming the Right Form Of Business for You

Just as the clothes you wear should fit your body, the form of your business should fit your personal goals and aspirations. There are three basic forms of business: sole proprietorship, partnership, and corporation. If you are an informal person, and you want to keep things simple in business, you may be perfectly suited to a proprietorship. If you and your spouse or mate are planning to work in the business together, or if you and another photographer are planning to set up a joint operation, then you need at least a partnership arrangement. But if you are risking several thousands of dollars on your business, and you don't want to expose your family to any greater risk, then perhaps you should incorporate.

Following is an overview of the three business forms.

Sole Proprietorship

The simplest and most common form of business in the United States is the **sole proprietorship.** This means *you* are the business. You are responsible for its assets and its liabilities. If it succeeds, you pay personal income taxes on the profits. If it fails, you pay for the losses out of your personal assets.

A major advantage in having a sole proprietorship is flexibility. You don't

have to worry about a corporate board member hounding you about a decision you have made. You can buy that tool you need when you want to, and you have the money to pay for it. You can accept an unusual job to bring in income this month, while you await the start of a long-term contract next month. And your bookkeeping is simple and straight-forward, because you don't have to worry about paying limited partners or corporate income taxes.

A major disadvantage of a sole proprietorship is liability. You can get sued for your business, your house, and your car. To help alleviate this liability, you can purchase insurance in the amount you need and can afford.

Partnership

Partnerships are like marriages: Some are great, and some are rocky from the start. A **partnership** is two or more people banding together to operate a business. In a general partnership, all partners share in profits, losses, and liabilities. The proportion is determined usually by the amount of each partner's investment and by his or her degree of involvement in the day-to-day business. In a partnership, you can be equal partners, or you can have a 60 percent/40 percent split, whatever your situation demands. In a limited partnership, certain partners restrict their liability to specific aspects of the business, spelled out in a written agreement.

A major advantage in a partnership, again, is flexibility. You can open your business doors with just an oral agreement between partners to share equally in everything. If you and your spouse are already working together and producing a business income, in the eyes of the Internal Revenue Service, you already are a partnership, whether you agreed to it or not.

A major disadvantage of partnerships is that you are still personally liable for your share of the losses and debts–even if your partner was the one who bought that machine you didn't really need.

As in most cases in business, it's a good idea when dealing with partners to "get it in writing." You may just need a simple partnership agreement, spelling out the investments, duties, profit and loss shares, and miscellaneous responsibilities of each partner. Even if your partner is your mate, a written checklist of duties and responsibilities will help to avoid confusion and hard feelings later.

A partnership agreement should do the following:

o Specify the amount and type of investment for each partner

o List specific responsibilities of each partner

o Quantify the amount of time each partner is to spend working in the business

o Specify how profits and losses will be shared

o Detail how a partner can withdraw from the partnership and what happens to that partner's share of the assets and liabilities

A critical factor in investments is the value of each partner's contribution. If each partner is investing the same amount of money, it's simple. But if one partner is investing money, and another is investing a combination of money and time, it's best to specify in writing what that time is worth, how it translates into splitting up the profits and losses.

For instance, Joe invests $3,000 and John, $1,500. John will do all the legwork to get the business started, while Joe continues working at his other job. John also will contribute his calculator and a desk to the partnership. Figuring John's labor at $15 per hour and the value of the calculator and desk at $250, John and Joe will be equal partners when John invests a little more than 83 hours of work in the project.

Usually, however, it's much more complicated, especially when it comes to tracking time investments and setting values on used equipment. Invariably, you invest more time than you charge to the partnership, just to get things off the ground. But if you can work through the intricacies of this phase of a partnership, you have a chance at working well together in business. On the other hand, if you're squabbling over whether a partner is reimbursed for a $20 book, then how will you handle buying a $2,000 custom-designed software package when you need it?

Corporation

A corporation sounds bigger, and it looks impressive to have "Inc." on your stationery. Your personal and business lives are separated by paperwork when you run your own **corporation.** Money for the business's services or products is paid to the corporation. The corporation then pays your salary and all of the operating expenses of the business. That includes paying you for the "rental" of office space in your home.

A major advantage of a corporation is lack of personal liability. If your business is sued for damages associated with a product defect, then your personal assets are protected. However, if you plan to borrow money as a new business—even though you're a corporation—many sources will require some degree of personal guarantee, in case the business fails.

The start-up costs of a corporation can be substantial and sometimes prohibitive, especially if your plunge into freelancing is due to an unexpected layoff. There are tax breaks, but the paperwork involved in a corporation also is considerable. Some states are "tax friendly," and others are not. And if you're so busy in the beginning that you just perform your work and don't do much of anything else, who is going to take care of the corporate paperwork?

A corporation consists of three main elements: a board of directors, a chief executive, and one or more stockholders. Sometimes they are all the same people. Sometimes, you might want someone who is not part of the everyday business to serve on the board. If you incorporate as a freelancer, you're more than likely going to be the chief executive, or president.

Although you can operate anywhere, you form a corporation within the jurisdiction of one of the 50 states. That's one of the reasons there's a lot of paperwork; each state treats corporations differently. You don't have to incorporate in the state in which you live; many businesses incorporate in those states that have the most favorable business laws. You should discuss incorporation with a professional accountant, lawyer, or both, before plunging ahead.

How much you spend on the incorporation process depends on how much of the work you do yourself. You can get an incorporation kit at an office-supply house for a few dollars, fill it out yourself, have it reviewed by a friendly attorney, pay your state's fees, and be incorporated for just a few hundred dollars. This is very time-consuming on your part. The other end of the spectrum is to let an attorney do all the work for you, which could easily cost more than $1,000, in addition to your state's fees. A third option is to have it done by a company that is specially set up to incorporate other companies. One of these is The Company Corporation, a Delaware firm that advertises it can incorporate your business in any state, with a variety of options and fees.

A subchapter S corporation offers tax advantages to small companies, but if you live in Connecticut, this form of incorporation is not recognized by the state.

Getting Down to Business

After you have determined the proper form for your business to take, you should determine what local and state

ZONING AND HOME-BASED BUSINESSES

So, you've decided that working at home, for whatever reason, is your best choice. You've had the family powwow, worked out the type of business it will be and the form it will take, ordered the fax machine, and had the second phone line installed. Your family has accepted the fact that you're going to be around the house all day long and that they will be losing a little of their freedom. You think that finally, just maybe, you have conquered the start-up beast. Maybe not.

Have you been to the town hall? Are you required to have a permit or a license to operate a business at home? If you are within the limitations of zoning requirements now, what will happen if you add an employee—even a part-time employee? Will you be breaking the law every morning when you sit down in front of your computer, turn on your band saw, or meet with a client in your shop? Maybe yes. Maybe no. Every town has its own unique set of zoning laws and regulations.

Zoning laws originally were set up to protect residential neighborhoods from encroachment by factories and smokestacks, sheepherders, blacksmiths, and chicken ranchers. And, while it may seem silly that anyone would object to you working at a computer in your spare room, different towns have different regulations, and it is always best to check with the local zoning office before ordering your business cards.

Towns usually divide land into four categories: residential, commercial, agricultural, and industrial. Those four categories are further divided: Single-family residential, multifamily residential, light industrial, and heavy industrial are but a few variations.

If your area's zoning laws allow home businesses, further restrictions apply as to how much of the home can be used for the business. Business space may be restricted to 25 percent or less of total floor space. This is to keep someone from renting or purchasing a home in your neighborhood and using it as a commercial bakery, while he lives either somewhere else or in one small area of the house. Also, certain occupations often are forbidden even in home-business zones due to the nature of the occupation, such as an auto-repair shop that specializes in maintaining race-car engines.

How many people will come to your house each day? Some areas restrict that number for home businesses. You can have a party in your house seven nights a week—as long as it's not a Tupperware party, which could be classified as a retail business if it became a regular, ongoing event. You can also have dozens of relatives driving in and out of the neighborhood, but watch out for the number of employees you have doing this. Figure out where the employees and customers will park, where your inventory will be stored, and whether or not you can construct a sign outside your house.

You can ignore the zoning regulations—not a recommended option—and you may never be caught. Or you can irritate a neighbor who knows where you work, and next thing you know, you get a call from the town's zoning officer. When your bread and butter depends on compliance with the law, it's always better to be safe than sorry. Hours, days, or even weeks spent battling the zoning commission means time not spent working, which, in accounting terms, is nonbillable time.

When your plans conflict with the zoning laws, you have to change your plans or the laws. Maybe you can rent an office or shop away from home, but that goes against your wishes to work at home. When feasible, your only solution may be to move to another area of town or to a different town all together. Remember, in the age of faxes and computers, many home-based occupations can be operated from any location that has electricity. But what do you do if your children are in high school; your mate's job has excellent benefits, including health insurance; and your home mortgage is only three years old, meaning you don't have a prayer of turning a profit, or possibly breaking even, if you sell. Sometimes, you can't pull up stakes and move. Sometimes, you have to fight city hall.

Many of the zoning laws were written long ago, before the days of computers. Many towns made across-the-board rulings forbidding home businesses with the hopes of keeping hair salons, retail stores, and auto-repair shops out of residential neighborhoods.

There are ways to change the laws, if you find that you are in violation, and it is best to do so before opening your business:

o First, stay friendly with your neighbors. Explain what type of business you are planning to operate. Tell them how many visitors, be it customers, clients, or employees, you will have in your house—and in their neighborhood—each day. Ask the neighbors to sign a petition requesting a variance to the zoning law.

o Second, try talking to as many members of the zoning commission as possible. It never hurts to have friends in high places. Just remember, zoning officers can be some of the most hated people in town, so you'll get farther with a positive attitude.

o Third, check the zoning regulations of neighboring towns. Possibly your area is the only one that forbids home-based businesses, and your zoning officials can be persuaded to change the law.

— Margaret Heinrich Hand

requirements exist. For some home-based occupations, a business license is required, but not for others. Some residential areas allow home-based businesses, others allow only certain types of home-based businesses, and some areas are extremely strict. For a look at **zoning,** see the box beginning on page 98.

Even if your home is properly zoned for the enterprise you want to pursue, other rules and regulations apply. Determining whether you need an occupational business license is only the beginning. For instance, you may need to file a fictitious, or assumed, name statement. The main test is whether your business name contains the full name of its owner. Harry Johnson, Editor would not need to file such a form, but Acme Miscellaneous Services would. The statement may need to be filed with your state, county, or locality. A check with local officials and possibly a chamber of commerce can help determine the requirements.

Specific agencies regulate certain types of businesses. A catering service would need to follow certain food-handling codes, administered by the public health department. Cupcakes-by-Mail would also need to follow mail-order regulations. And many professions, regardless of where the office is located, require a professional certification.

To determine whether you need to charge sales tax, contact your state revenue department and get them to send you an application and information on getting a **tax identification number.** In the past, most people thought sales tax only applied to merchandise, some tangible item you buy at a retail store and take

home to use. But with states searching for funds to finance schools and build roads for growing populations, services have come under the purview of sales tax. Each state is a little different, and you'll have to make your own determination.

Along with the state tax identification number, you'll need a federal employer tax identification number. You'll need this even if you are the only worker in your business, and you are a sole proprietorship. The number is used by the federal government to track payroll deductions and withholding taxes, but it also is the number you give the bank when you open your business checking account. This means that any transactions in your account that are reported to the government are reported under the business name, not under your Social Security number.

If you have employees, even part-time ones, you will need to carry worker's compensation insurance. This can be quite expensive, depending on the type of work your worker does. Insurance for a receptionist is not nearly as high as insurance for a bungee-jumping demonstrator. A broader discussion on insurance is offered in Chapter 10.

Making Sure Independent Means Independent

One legal trap you definitely want to avoid is the misclassification of any workers you hire as independent contractors, when they are really employees. The IRS has been extremely aggressive about this in recent years, because it feels that too many companies are evading payroll taxes by calling employees "independent contractors." As a freelancer, you're an independent contractor, too, so you need to be aware of the laws regulating this aspect of your life. If someone is trying to use you as an employee, let them do so honestly. On the other hand, if you subcontract some of your work to another freelancer, make sure the work and pay arrangements are clear.

Some of the disadvantages you assume when you freelance are some of the advantages in hiring other freelancers. You don't have to pay Social Security taxes or worker's compensation insurance or provide health insurance to another freelancer. But you just can't call somebody an independent contractor to escape employer expenses. The IRS has specific guidelines for differentiating between the two. Violating the rules can result in severe assessments of back taxes plus penalties, often in amounts high enough to bankrupt a small company and cause a personal catastrophe for a sole proprietor.

When it comes to playing 20 questions, the IRS really does. When it questions a business about independent contractors, the IRS asks how the contractor fares under 20 different criteria. The IRS uses the test, based on common law, to determine the following:

1. The extent of instructions offered by the employer to the worker
2. The extent of training offered by the employer to the worker
3. How the worker's services are used by the employer
4. Whether the worker personally provides the services
5. Whether the worker offers his/her services to the general public
6. Whether the worker can make or lose money on the deal
7. Whether the worker can quit at any time without being liable for anything
8. Whether the worker can be fired at any time by the employer
9. If the sequence of work is determined by the employer
10. Who owns the tools the worker uses
11. Whether the worker follows prescribed hours of work
12. Whether the worker can employ workers of his/her own
13. If the relationship between worker and employer is continuous
14. Whether the worker works for one employer at a time
15. If the employer pays the worker regularly, based on time worked
16. If the employer pays for business and travel expenses incurred by the worker
17. If the worker is working full-time for the employer
18. If the worker is working on the employer's premises
19. If the worker does not have a significant investment in facilities used to perform his/her work
20. If the worker has to submit regular reports to the employer

If too many of the answers to these questions point to a high degree of control or supervision by the employer, the IRS is inclined to classify the worker as an employee. As a freelancer, you can subcontract for a specified amount of work by a specified date at a specified quality, but when you start telling the subcontractor when to work and in what sequence to do each task, you start to cross the legal boundary.

Putting It in Writing

For subcontracting and other purposes, you may need one or more standard **contract** forms for your business. Some of these are available in office-supply stores, including such forms as model releases for photographers and repair orders for service technicians. Others are available on various computer software offerings. But if you require a special contract, or need to modify a standard contract to meet your individual needs, it is a good idea to get an attorney to at least review the contract, if not prepare it.

There are a few things you, as a freelancer, need to have in every contract, however—whether you are the person doing the hiring or the person doing the work. The basic elements are

o Names and signatures
o Dates (for signing, beginning work, ending work, and any progress dates)
o Scope of services
o Explanation of payments
o Method of cancellation
o Method of returning any funds or property exchanged if the contract is terminated

o A clause that protects you if the work is stopped in progress through no fault of your own
o A clause that explains what will happen if the work is late

You may have a number of other elements that apply to your specific business. If you discuss your concerns with a lawyer and get a good contract in the beginning, then the money you spend up front will pay for itself over and over.

Protecting Your Assets

One of the legal priorities you should establish as a freelancer is to make a will that sets forth what should be done with your business in the event of your death, particularly if you are working as a proprietorship or in a partnership. A will should specify what happens to your business assets and how your business liabilities will be handled. In the case of a partnership, you also may need to include a clause on whom, if anyone, can assume operation of your share of the partnership, although this should be spelled out in your partnership agreement.

For now, protecting your assets is a matter of controlling the quality of your work; keeping the business honest; forming solid contracts; and insuring what you can afford to insure, including yourself. Key insurance considerations are

o Getting a home-business rider on your renter's or homeowner's policy, including enough liability to protect you against a client's potential injury, and getting insurance on your equipment

○ Obtaining a disability policy on yourself

○ Maintaining at least a catastrophic health-care policy

○ Making sure your automobile insurance covers you if you use your car in business

Don't Let the Tax Man Get You

Taxes make up the final element of this chapter. You can't escape them; you have to deal with them sooner or later. As a freelancer, you'll be responsible for paying self-employment taxes, which make up for the Social Security contributions an employer would have made in your name. Typically, as long as you make money, you pay self-employment tax and regular income tax in quarterly installments, called estimated taxes. The installments are due April 15, July 15, October 15, and January 15; each date falls 15 days after the end of the quarter on which you were taxed.

If you have full- or part-time employees, you have to deduct and pay federal income taxes on them, plus make contributions to their Social Security accounts and pay unemployment taxes. You can obtain all the necessary forms for this from the IRS.

Don't forget the state and locality either. You may have to pay estimated state income taxes and deduct and pay state income taxes on any employees you have. Many localities also assess property taxes on business property.

There are so many varieties of taxes, it's hard to know what you need to file by when, unless you consult an accountant. The main thing is to stay up-to-date on all your taxes, because penalties often make late payments prohibitive. Besides, from a legal standpoint, tax agencies are the last group you want being suspicious of your activities.

CHAPTER TEN

Money and Motives

KEY TERMS

budget

financing

overhead

cash flow

home-office deduction

profit

A full-time freelancer must make a profit. Otherwise, unless there's a rich relative willing to provide unlimited, unencumbered grants, you're out of business. Making that profit involves not just selling and providing competent service or quality products; it also involves spending your business money wisely.

Shopping around for health insurance can save you hundreds of dollars a month. Also, try to pay your taxes correctly and on time, because once you get behind, it's extremely difficult to catch up. The money you pay out in late-tax penalties could be better spent on new equipment, the cost of which you can depreciate to lower your taxes. In your work, proper analysis of your time and efforts will tell you if you need to hone your pricing skills. And it's absolutely essential that you get your clients to pay on time by using proper invoicing, constant communication, and, if necessary, effective collection techniques.

To help you do all of the above, keep accurate, up-to-date records on what you're earning and what you're spending. Develop a system to keep personal and business use of your home separate. Depending on the form of your business, this can mean just taking a home-office deduction on your federal tax return or having your business account pay for apportioned home expenses.

The Profit Motive

While **profit** is a dirty word to some people, it's not something a freelancer should shun. If you truly believe in yourself as a freelancer, then profit is what will allow you to continue doing what you are doing. Just meeting expenses gets you by from month to month, but having some profit left over will allow you to exercise more control over your own future.

To gain a proper perception of profit, freelancers need to consider two things. First, they need to take a hard look at what service or product they provide, how well they do their work, and how timely they deliver it. Second, they have to consider how valuable their service or product is to their customers or clients. Determine what dollar figure you need to produce one unit of your service or product. Now, compare that price with what you think your service or product is worth to the buyer. The latter figure can be considered "what the market will bear." And the difference between the two is the arena in which you set your profit margin.

A profit margin is necessary in your pricing, because it determines such things as how much your business grows, whether you have enough money to finance a vacation, or whether you can buy a new piece of equipment. Companies operate on a wide range of profit margins, from 1 percent to 100 percent or more, depending on whether they are service-oriented or product-oriented, and depending on what their competitors are doing. A competitive supermarket may have to reduce its prof-it margin to 1 percent on a high-volume commodity, such as seasonal fruit, to stay competitive against the store across the street. Profit margin is one factor you, as a freelancer, can adjust to meet the competition's pricing. But unless you can match a supermarket in sales volume, it's not safe to get too close to the 1 percent mark. More palatable figures are 10 percent, 15 percent, and up.

Establishing a Pricing Schedule

A hair-color commercial on television, where the blonde actress claims to use such-'n'-such hair color, can teach freelancers an important aspect of selling their service or product: perception of worth. It may cost a little more, the actress says about the hair color, but "I'm worth it." Getting to know your worth as a freelancer, and then exploiting that, will put you on a strong financial footing. Some freelancers labor under the impression that if they don't work for mega corporation, they must not be as good as the people who do. So they charge the bare minimum to get by. They are destined to look around 20 years from now, if they're still in business, and wonder, Where did I go wrong?

Freelancers are not nonprofit organizations. They, just like the mega corporation, are entitled to a profit. And while you don't have the overhead of an office outside your house, you do have expenses, many times at a rate higher than that charged to the larger companies. Setting up a fee schedule involves analyzing expenses and building in a profit margin.

So, how do you figure out what to charge? The simplest way to start is to determine how much you want to make. Divide that figure by the number of weeks and hours you will work, and you should come up with an hourly rate for yourself. If you want to gross at least $45,000 in the first year and take two weeks' vacation and 10 holidays off, you would begin this way:

$45,000 ÷ 48 weeks = $937.50 per week

$937.50 ÷ 40 hours = $23.44 per hour

But if you count 40 hours a week as billable time—time that you can bill a client as a direct result of work done on a project—when will you fit in the marketing, the bookkeeping, the downtime because of computer problems, and the time spent searching for and purchasing tools and supplies? It's time to recalculate your hourly rate based on what you think you can bill out:

$937.50 ÷ 30 hours = $31.25 per hour

Looks Are Deceiving

At that rate, you would have to bill clients for at least 1,440 hours of work, or 69 percent of the 2,080 work hours in a 40-hour, 52-week period, to gross $45,000. But—*there's always a but*—how did you arrive at the $45,000 figure in the first place? Is that what you grossed on your last day job? Is that what you need in cold hard cash to keep the bills paid, save a few dollars, contribute to your child's college fund, and still have

enough left over for that two-week vacation? Is that what you need to just pay the bills? If so, you're still thinking like an employee and not a freelancer.

You have to figure in the direct and indirect costs of doing business. Direct costs are easier to calculate. You spent $300 on photographs, $750 on printing, and $150 on shipping and handling to produce and mail a brochure for an advertising client. You simply add the $1,200 to your labor charge, and you have a base price to charge your client. But to get a fair price for you, you need to add in overhead and profit.

Overhead expenses include fixed costs, such as the mortgage payment, which is the same every month, and indirect costs for services and items that are consumed as part of the business but that are not tied to one project. Those indirect costs include the time you spend on bookkeeping and marketing and the cost of toner cartridges and paper for the laser printer, the business stationery, banking services, advertising, basic telephone service, electricity, and extra taxes you have to pay as a self-employed person or business. You can only estimate these expenses before you start business. But after you're up and running, it's important to track the costs on a regular basis, so you can adjust the overhead factor in pricing. For an example of overhead expenses, see the chart on page 108.

Granted, you will have a tax advantage in owning your own business that you didn't have as someone else's employee. Still, you have to actually make the money and actually incur the expenses before you get the tax advan-

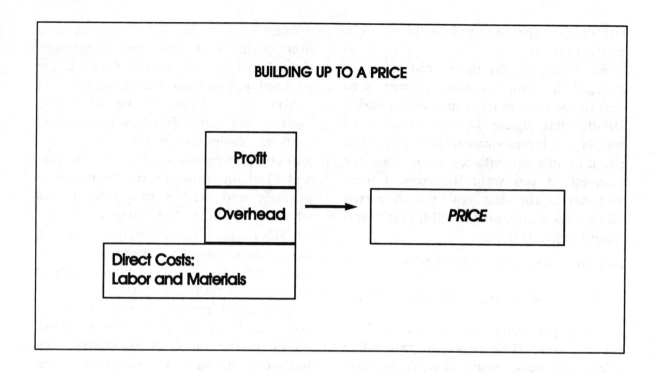

BUILDING UP TO A PRICE

tages. And if you price your products and services too low, your expenses will overwhelm you.

To get an overall look at your pricing, you can fall back on a traditional formula:

direct costs (materials and labor)
+ overhead + profit = price.

Your figure of $937.50 a week corresponds to the labor portion of the direct costs. That's because an employer would cover the direct and indirect expenses and realize the profit. So, to get a true price for your products or services, you'll have to add direct costs, overhead, and profit.

For example, if your overhead is $125 a week, and you want to make a profit of 15 percent, a week's work might look like this:

$937.50 labor
+ $85 materials
= $1,022.50 direct costs

$1,022.50 direct costs
+ $125 overhead
= $1,147.50 total costs

$1,147.50 total costs
x 15%
= $172.13 profit

$1,147.50 total costs
+ $172.13 profit
= $1,319.63 total price to charge

Now it's time to reset your hourly billing rate. Using your 30-hour projection for billable time, the above pricing works out to about $44 per hour as your billing rate ($1,319.63 total price ÷ 30 hours = $44 per hour). But are you sure you will be busy enough and efficient enough to bill out 30 hours a week, every week? How many days of sick leave did you take last year? Do you have enough work lined up to fill your calendar? To play it safe, and keep an eye toward cash flow, you can figure in an efficiency factor and a fluctuation factor.

Maybe because of computer problems and a funeral in the family, you lost a day of billable time last month. Twenty working days a month minus one day lost equals a 5 percent efficiency factor. Maybe the contract you had counted on didn't materialize because the other company went out of business or had a fire. That particular job was going to last a total of three weeks, although you had scheduled it, along with other jobs, over a seven-week period. Forty-eight working weeks in a year minus three lost weeks equals more than 6 percent in a fluctuation factor. These factors will, of course, vary according to the type of business and the economic climate. But even if you gain another client to compensate for the lost one, you still have to figure your overhead for the time it took to find the new client and adjust the schedule.

So, if you take your original 30-hour projection for billable time and reduce it by 11 percent—the total of the efficiency and fluctuation factors—you get a revised projection of 26.7 hours of billable time per week. Based on the above $937.50 a week in personal income, plus $382.13 in expenses, overhead, and profit, you would have a total weekly billing of $1,319.63 to be charged against 26.7 hours of work. That yields an hourly rate of $49.42. You can see immediately why $50 an hour is a common rate for some services. Other services, however, can command much higher rates, depending on the expertise needed and the market.

Assess Where You Fit Into the Market

Now, take a look at what you will be doing as a freelancer. If others are doing it locally, how much do they charge and how much do they make? Does your initial estimate fall within the market's range? If you are providing a service, are there enough clients out there willing to pay you what you're worth to bring in that $900 per week or more? Hopefully, you discovered the answers to these types of questions when you were doing the research described in Chapter 5, "When the Market Will Bear It". Have you priced yourself out of a job before you even started? If you're trying to make $45,000 a year, but others in your business make $30,000, you have some choices:

o Do more and better work than your competitor

o Lower your financial expectations

o Market yourself better than your competitor does

o Broaden the scope, professionally or geographically, of what you do

However, if you find that competitors in your field have a broad range of incomes, from $30,000 to $100,000, then there's a good chance you will at least earn your minimum expected income—and possibly more. Now comes the fun part, actually doing the work and getting paid for it.

If you are providing a service, your fees are often determined by the buyers of your service. Writers, for instance, don't often tell publishers what to pay for a magazine article. It's usually the other way around, unless the writer is one of the few who can actually set his or her own fees. When you are working under these circumstances, you control your income by the efficiency and volume of your work. If you are getting $1,000 for every magazine article, can you research, write, *sell, and get paid for* an average of one article per week to reach your goal of earning $45,000 the first year?

If you're a consultant, you may actually be paid on an hourly basis. However, some arrangements call for a flat project fee or a cost-plus-fee formula. Arriving at hourly consulting fees involves more than just determining what you want to make in a year. If you've checked out your competitors, or had occasion to hire other consultants in your last job, you know how much they charge, so you know what the market will bear. At that point, you can set your fee based on your aspirations and the market.

When bidding on a long-term job, however, don't forget to add in your overhead, the profit margin, and the sometimes easy-to-forget expenses, such as numerous long-distance faxes, overnight parcel shipping, extra travel expenses, and special research costs. Also, some consultants bill for travel

time, too. After all, it is time they may not use otherwise, except possibly read or study if they're traveling by train or plane. The rate for travel time varies, with 50 percent of the normal fee being a common price.

If you are making a product instead of providing a service, consider how much, or how many pieces, you can make in a week. Total up the direct costs of the materials and labor used to make the products, using the 30-hour figure you calculated above to get your hourly labor rate. Add to that overhead and profit. Divide the total figure by the number of units you can make in a week to arrive at a unit price. The formula would look like this:

direct costs (material and labor) + overhead + profit = gross price

gross price ÷ number of units
= unit price

If you're a baker, you may want to develop a specialty cake business. Not only would you need to consider the cost of the ingredients—flour, sugar, oil, eggs, and flavorings—but you would also include your overhead, such as wear and tear on your appliances and the cost of electricity, the mortgage, and the telephone. Now, suppose that you can make 4 cakes a day, five days a week, which equals 20 cakes a week. You spend $40 a week in direct supplies, and your overhead is $125. Your skills as a baker are worth $500 a week in labor costs, and you want to build in 15 percent profit.

If the cakes are the only thing you do in a week, you would set your initial pricing as follows:

$40 material costs + $125 overhead + $500 labor costs = $665 total costs

$665 total costs x 15% = $99.75 profit

$665 + $99.75 = $764.75 total costs and profit

$764.75 ÷ 20 cakes = $38.24 per cake

That's $38.24 *per* cake. If that is in line with your area's prices, or if you think the market will bear that price for a specialty cake that nobody else bakes, then you're in business. But remember, if the local commercial bakery on Main Street downtown can make the same product for half the price, your expectations and rates may be unrealistic. You may have to lower your profit or add some type of service to your product, such as free home delivery. That additional service would increase your costs, of course, but it might just be the marketing tool you need to get your business off the ground and running.

Your Money or Theirs?

A prime question for freelancers is where to get the money to start your business. There are almost as many ways to raise money as there are different types of freelancing occupations. In many cases, freelancers finance their own ventures, especially if they have never owned a business before, since lenders tend to look upon them as bad risks. You may withdraw savings, cash in a certificate of deposit, or take a severance package from your former employer to pay for start-up costs and provide for the first few months

of operation. You may be lucky enough to land a freelance contract that pays you an advance, which you can then use for your start-up. This is obviously more risky—financially and professionally—than having a specific start-up fund.

Some **financing** options include borrowing from relatives, getting a personal bank loan, charging equipment and computers on your credit cards, and getting a home-equity loan. You may be able to establish a line of credit with a commercial bank, then borrow only what you need as you need it. If your business is sophisticated enough, you may raise capital by incorporating and selling stock. Chapter 12 contains a discussion of various levels of financing, based on the degree to which you pursue freelancing. For the purposes of this chapter, however, it is assumed that you have a start-up fund, and you just want to get on with business.

Budget Isn't a Dirty Word

Nothing goes faster than money when you're starting a business, except maybe the time it takes to spend it. That's why it's important to have a **budget.** Before you launch into full-time freelancing, you should develop a start-up budget. Then, you'll need some kind of operating budget on which you base day-to-day decisions regarding income and expenses. You can make these budgets as simple or elaborate as you need.

Your start-up budget should include the amount of capital you have to invest in the business and how you plan to spend it. Include all the items on the list you developed when deciding how to equip your office or shop (see Chapter 8). Also include legal and accounting expenses, license fees, travel costs, special research expenses, and promotional expenses. Don't forget the costs of setting up a business bank account, including the price of having checks and deposit slips printed.

Once you develop your first start-up budget, put it away for a day or two, then revisit it to see what you forgot to include and to reevaluate whether you really need to buy everything on the list. There will be certain things that you absolutely have to have to open your business, other things that you would like to have, and others that would be nice but aren't necessary. Make sure you plan for and get everything you need, because if you don't have the tools necessary to perform the work, you can't produce an income. But if you can pare down the nice-but-not-necessary list in the start-up budget, you'll have more money to put into the daily operation of the business and to pay for unplanned expenses.

The basic ingredients of a simple operating budget are income, expenses, and profit. Generally, you establish a monthly budget, which you can summarize into a yearly budget. But, if you generate income on a daily or weekly basis, you may have short-term ledger sheets that you use to monitor day-to-day progress. While it's only necessary to write the expenses and amounts on a budget sheet, some people find it beneficial to also include the date on which a certain item is due. You can then incorporate the budget into your monthly calendar.

When developing a budget, write everything possible down. It's common to underestimate expenses and be disappointed after a month in business. After you list everything, take another look. Perhaps one of the expenses you listed will remind you that before you can buy a new file cabinet, you have to pay last month's credit card bill for the computer software. If you don't have expenses written down, you tend to forget they exist, especially when your mind is concentrating on all the other details of freelancing.

Tracking expenses as you incur them is important, too. Write down what you spend, when and where you spend it, for what, and whether it was a budgeted item. If it wasn't in your budget, how will it affect your being able to meet your planned expenses?

Home-Based Considerations

When working in your home, or when your home is the base of your operation, special considerations exist regarding expenses. If you're a sole proprietor, you may take the **home-office deduction** when filing your income taxes, or you may pay yourself rent on the space that the business occupies. Specific conditions have to be met before taking the home-office tax deduction, and this is a point you should discuss with your accountant. The rules also have been subject to change over the past few years, so make sure you get the latest interpretation.

In general, to qualify for the deduction, the home office has to be a specifically defined area of your home. It also has to be the primary location you use to produce the income the deduction is against. Another consideration is depreciation. While you can benefit in the short-term from depreciating part of your residence, it may be detrimental if you sell your home and have to recapture the depreciation.

Whether you take the home-office deduction or pay yourself rent, just don't forget to include the related expenses in your budgeting and planning. If your home office or shop consumes 15 percent of your residence, for instance, count 15 percent of the related expenses in your business budget. Otherwise, your pricing and fee setting will not accurately reflect your expenses.

Keeping Expenses in Line

Controlling expenses is related to risk taking in many ways. The more you risk, the less you may have to spend up front, and you take your chances on the consequences. Below are some of the ways you can keep expenses in line:

o By buying only catastrophic health insurance. This will cost hundreds less per month than a health maintenance organization.

o By buying high-deductible health insurance. This lessens your exposure to such occurrences as a broken arm developing complications that are expensive to treat but that are not catastrophic. You can set your deductible at the point where you're most comfortable, from $250 to $2,000 per person.

o By raising the deductible on your car insurance. Again, set it to a comfortable point.

o By buying in bulk. Office supplies, particularly, are cheaper by the dozen. If you plan properly, you can save money by buying such things as copy paper in as large a quantity as you can afford, then budgeting the expense over a longer period of time. This also depends, however, on how much storage space you have in your home.

o By shopping around for telephone service. The big telephone companies are highly competitive, but you have to really analyze the details of their offers before deciding which one will save your business money.

o By concentrating on public relations instead of advertising. If you depend on the public as a source of income, you need a positive image to keep the income growing. Advertising can get expensive. So, get as much free publicity as possible (see Chapter 11).

o By doing your own bookkeeping. If your business is simple enough for you to do your own bookkeeping, you'll save hundreds of dollars a year. But if the bookkeeping is such a chore that it takes valuable time away from your main income-generating occupation, then this is not a good option.

A tricky aspect of controlling expenses is how much effect they have on your overall job performance. Remember when you worked late at the office and your call telling your family when you'd be home was always interrupted by the people in the cleaning service? That service was an expense to your employer, but it also meant that during regular work hours, employees would concentrate on their work and not on having to take out the garbage or vacuum the floor. As a freelancer, you should look at such things with a business eye.

You may feel guilty that laundry is piling up as both you and your spouse work hard and put in extra hours to meet a tight deadline. You have to relax sometimes, too. Having a cleaning service come into your house, as often as you can afford it, may make better sense than doing the chores yourself, especially when the income from one or two hours of work can more than offset the price of the cleaning service.

You may also feel that the on-line computer service you subscribe to charges too much for downloading magazine articles or has too many service fees for forums or user groups. To gauge whether your feeling is accurate, compare the cost of the service to the time and expense of going to the library to do the research, or of talking long-distance to one of the people in your network of associates.

Freelancing and Personal Debt

Whether you're leaping or being pushed into freelancing may have an effect on your money management considerations. If you've been planning the move for quite a while, you've made provisions for paying off credit cards and clearing up department store accounts. You'll be able to concentrate on building the business with all the spare cash you can muster. But if you are about to be or have been cast into the vat of freelancing because of downsizing or other economic factors, you may not be so lucky in the area of personal debt. When you were employed, you didn't worry about not having money to pay credit card bills, and you preferred not to think about the interest you were paying.

If you are the latter person, take a serious look at what you owe and develop a reasonable plan to handle your debt, while you build the business. Confronting the issue in the beginning will help to alleviate chronic worry about paying the bills, and instead you'll be able to concentrate on getting more clients to sign up with you. If you need to, consult an accountant or debt counselor to get advice.

Some management strategies include converting one or more credit cards to lower-interest cards. But many of the low-interest offers have limited time frames, and unless you can pay off the balance within that time, you may not save any money over the long term. Also, take into account which cards charge annual fees. It may be possible to consolidate all of your bills into one loan or onto one lower-interest card. Another strategy is to use one card just for business. That way, if any interest accumulates, it is tax-deductible.

Record Keeping and Computer Software

Speaking of deductions, you can't take them if you don't record them. It is critical that you keep, or arrange for a bookkeeper to keep, thorough and accurate records of your business income and expenses. Your bookkeeping system should also have a method of keeping receipts. You can't deduct expenses that you forgot you had. And it's risky to deduct expenses if you don't have proof of purchase.

For home-based freelancers, an important part of the record keeping involves tracking the business portion of your home expenses. This is usually done on a percentage basis. In a six-room house, it is fair to charge one-sixth of the rent and utilities as office expenses. When you use the family car for company business, note the mileage. If you drive 20,000 miles a year and 10,000 of those miles are for company business, you can charge half of your car expenses to the business.

Basic bookkeeping considerations include:

o If you are short on time and short on money for a bookkeeper, too, you might consider getting a credit card—or using one you already have—for the business and charging many of the regular operating expenses to the card. Once a month, you get an already organized record of your expenses, and some cards supply a year-end tally as well.

o Keeping a business checking account to pay business expenses is a good idea, although it is not absolutely necessary if you are a sole proprietor and your business name is your own name. Check with local banks for the best account for your needs.

o Keep ALL of your business receipts. If you take a client out for coffee while

you discuss business, save the receipt and write the client's name on the back of the receipt. With 365 days in a year, it's difficult to remember why you saved particular receipts unless you write notes on the backs of them.

o If you don't want to track miscellaneous expense receipts as you incur them, pick a drawer or box to keep them in until you can set aside some time to record them. However, this should not be subject to a too flexible schedule. Making yourself do it once a week or month keeps you up-to-date.

The type of bookkeeping system you should use will depend on the type of business you're in and the type of business person you are. Even if you hate computers, you may want to consider an accounting software package for your business. The packages come in all levels of user-friendliness and complexity. The advantages are that you'll be prompted to think about filling in all the necessary details, and hopefully you won't have to spend hours sitting under a lamp writing numbers on columnar pads. Just remember, computers and computer disks fail, so make sure you have a backup copy of your records.

Managing the Cash Flow

How you set your fees, how much you budget for start-up, how you keep your books, and how you control your expenses all relate to that ever-present freelancing problem called **cash flow.** If you've never had to manage cash flow before, it may be one of the most diffi-

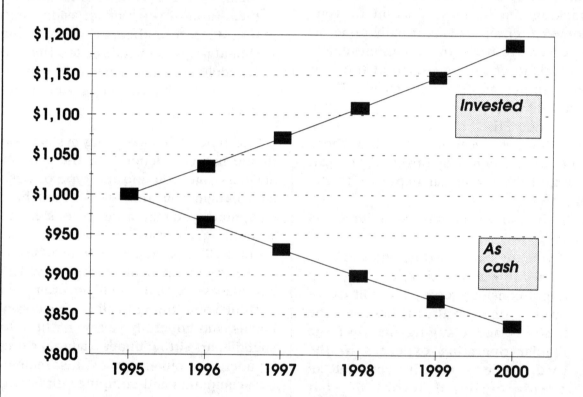

WHAT'S $1,000 WORTH?

If you put $1,000 in a checking account that earns no interest and let the money sit there for five years, you would have the equivalent of $836.83 at the end of the period if the average annual inflation rate was 3.5%. Apply that 3.5% rate as an average annual return on investment after inflation to the same $1,000, reinvesting the interest, and you would end up with $1,187.69 after five years.

cult freelancing skills to master. It's not a synonym for petty cash. It involves your checking account, your whole business, and your reputation with suppliers and lenders.

You can have a negative cash flow and still be profitable, or you can have a positive cash flow and still lose money. Essentially, managing cash flow means you have to have enough money on hand to meet day-to-day expenses. To do that, you have to plan for the future, monitor the present, and analyze the past.

If you're just starting out, you can only project what your cash flow requirements are going to be. Take your budget and calendar in hand and develop a projection as far into the future as you can. A year is usually the recommended period. Write down the amount of money you have at the start, then record the amounts you expect to take in and the dates on which you expect to receive the income. Now, write down the expenses you expect to incur and the dates on which you expect to spend the money.

Using a computer spreadsheet application is helpful in this, because it allows you to make adjustments easily and see various options quickly. The software also can put your figures in the form of a graph or chart very quickly, so you get a visual image of your projections. However, you may be more comfortable sitting down with a 13-column pad of paper and a mechanical pencil. In either case, you can use 12 columns for the months of the year and the 13th column for the yearly total.

Looking over your projected figures, you'll probably notice that in June, for example, you still have all of your monthly expenses plus a renewal payment on your car insurance, but you don't show enough income to cover everything. In April, you expect to have a few extra dollars, which you were planning to use to buy a new tool. This extra money should be just enough–hopefully–to make up the shortage in June. But in August, you show a whopping balloon payment due on a bank note. Can it be renegotiated? If so, how much will you need to pay on it, and when should you make the balloon payment due? You may have to carry more cash forward from July, rather than pulling it out of the checking account and buying a certificate of deposit.

It is important to plan for cash flow. After you're in business, you can use your record-keeping system to help you continually plan. You may find that what you had projected for income in July actually arrived in June. That made June a highly profitable month, but what does this do to the rest of the summer? Can you put some of the June money in a short-term investment and earn interest before you have to use the money for expenses in July, or is it just enough to carry you through August and not enough to offset penalties for early withdrawals?

Freelancing is a way of life and a business manifested in the form of cash flow.

CHAPTER ELEVEN

Yes, You Have to Sell— And Keep Selling

KEY TERMS

civic club   *follow-up*
homegrown ingenuity   *image*
research   *target*

Selling, whether you're in the service or product business, is a basic ingredient of success. You have to use whatever marketing techniques work best for your freelancing business. Selling successfully requires a comprehensive approach to your freelancing. It involves analyzing what you have to offer, to whom you want to offer it, and how much you want to be paid for it. It also involves planning for future sales, based on your past successes and failures. Some home-based businesses lend themselves very well to some of the same marketing techniques used by retail businesses. But you may also have to resort to some **homegrown ingenuity** to increase sales.

Big corporations rely on marketing surveys and intricately planned advertising and public relations campaigns. They also spend a fortune on it. Freelancers working out of their homes don't have that kind of money. Typically, you have to rely on your own unscientific, underfunded, and unadulterated **research.** You can buy a number of books that will tell you how to design and use a marketing plan. These textbooks cover all the basic principles involved in marketing businesses and products. But freelancing is more than a textbook business; it's more business-with-an-attitude than business-by-the-books. You can approach marketing with the attitude that you're going to reduce it to its most manageable level, then build it up to your own specifications.

In the Beginning . . .

Start out with the basics:
o What you sell
o To whom
o By what means

Then, explore your options. You will need to find the right audience for you and your product or service. After you identify your audience, however, you may have to devise various ways of reaching them and meeting their changing needs. Marketing and freelancing can then combine to form one evolutionary process, in which you develop new and additional buyers for new and additional products or services. Then again, your freelancing may be simpler, at least for a while, if you have a product that is a natural for a specific market, as illustrated in the following example.

If you're a woodworker, you could approach the basics this way:
o What you sell are highly polished wooden benches with intricately carved legs.
o You want to sell the benches to craft collectors who know the value of handmade furniture and don't mind paying for it.
o You think craft shows will be your best avenue for sales.

But *which* craft shows?

Consider your product again. Does it sell for $50, $250, or $1,000? You have priced it at $1,200, based on the cost of labor and materials plus overhead plus profit. Overhead would include time invested in bookkeeping, marketing, and travel to craft shows. You save some time due to efficiency in the shop—taking an assembly line approach, making a bunch of tops one day, rough-sawing a bunch of legs the next. But you also invest serious time on the delicate and slightly different carvings you put on each table's legs.

The $1,200 price range will be in the bleachers, even out of the ball park, for some craft shows. But it may be right in the midrange at upscale events that draw regional crowds and commercial buyers. You can attend one, two, or three of these shows in a year, and you might not have to leave the shop the rest of the year. You can make arrangements to sell your benches in craft or craft/art galleries through the buyers or gallery owners you meet at the shows. The shows are still your avenue for sales, but all of a sudden, you've discovered a side street as well.

Marketing a Service

Marketing a service can be more difficult. A craft collector can readily see the $1,200 worth of the woodworker's bench—which may even increase in value if the woodworker limits his production and becomes a guru to other woodworkers (that's another step in marketing). But if you're an advertising agent, convincing a retailer to let you handle all of her advertising becomes an exercise in public relations for yourself. You have to show the retailer you're a boy scout (honest and trustworthy), a professional (competent in your work), a plotter (you put the right ads in the right places), a leader (you devise new approaches and concepts), and a follower (you follow your instincts *and* the results of your research).

To start with the basics in this case, as an independent advertising agent you might take the following approach:

○ What you sell is a range of services: research into the best media for clients' ads, writing ad copy, designing newspaper and magazine ads, developing local television ad concepts, and placing and coordinating ads.

○ You want to sell your services to a range of clients, because you want to protect your income base during rocky economic times. The Smith family that runs the corner grocery store probably will be steady, but not overly lucrative, clients. Everybody has to eat, and the Smiths run a popular, locally owned store. The local manufacturing plant, which ships die-cast metal machine parts around the country and is about to start exporting, could be a lucrative account. But this account could also be cut back drastically if the world economy shifts.

○ Your method of selling is direct. You make appointments, make a presentation, and ask them to sign on the dotted line.

As you can see, the "basics" in this case lead to quite a few options to explore. As in the woodworker example, the product will be the constant in this example. The options will focus on the two other variables: who the customers are and how you sell to them.

The advertising clients listed are excellent bets for business, but possibly at two extremes of the income spectrum. You have stability; local appeal; and a basic, straightforward commodity—the grocery store—to advertise. The Smiths are good for about $100 a month in profit after expenses. The machine-parts plant is the other side of the coin. With a mission to expand and participate in a vigorous export market, the company needs research on foreign publications and media, on business publications that go to import/export brokers, and on what its potential competitors are advertising. Then it needs ads that hit its targets. You stand to gain a client worth thousands of dollars in profit over a few weeks' time.

But after you do all the initial research and write and place a series of ads, the manufacturer may want to sit back and see how effective the campaign is. At that point, you have to identify other potential clients. You start by reading a range of publications, from local newspapers to technical trade journals to your own advertising-trade publications. Pick out companies that are mentioned in articles, look for trends you can take advantage of, and monitor ads that are placed by companies you think could use help in their advertising.

If you have a list of clients and potential clients, how do you get appointments with them? You can try the direct approach by just calling or writing and asking for an appointment. If only it were that easy all the time. You can also convince the Smiths who own the grocery store to mention your name to their produce supplier, who just bought a controlling interest in an orchard and needs to get the word out to retailers. Another approach is to join a local **civic club** and attend its meetings regularly. In doing so, you'll meet other active business people on a regular basis. They will be potential customers, themselves, and they will know others who are not in the club, who may be potential customers, as well. If they see you at the meetings all the time, they come to trust you and are not afraid to either listen to your pitch or refer your name to another person.

Business men and women, especially the self-employed, often are involved in some way with the community. They belong to the Lions Club, the Rotary Club, the Jaycees, the Chamber of Commerce, you name it. Most of them would be in the clubs even if they weren't independent business people. But the clubs are a good way to network with other business leaders in town.

You have the appointment. Now, which presentation do you make. If you've been an advertising copywriter a few years, you'll have a portfolio to show and a track record to cite. But you didn't do any selling when you worked for an employer. So now you need to analyze your own advertising needs. You should **target** your portfolio and presentation to the particular client you're going to see, which means not showing a *Playboy* ad to a religious bookstore owner and other not-so-obvious restraints. Keep your presentation on a level that is suitable to the client. If the appointment is in a formal meeting room with two or three people listening, show up in an appropriate business suit and present a well-timed presentation. If the appointment is at the sidewalk cafe, over nachos and margaritas, dress appropriately and keep your presentation informal and flexible, but perhaps take your notebook computer with you in case you have to look up some information in a database.

The Never-ending Story— Finding and Keeping Customers

Even when you have an existing client or customer base, your marketing does not end there. Once you've got them, you've got to keep them. Perhaps your freelancing trade will be a once in a lifetime job per customer. Perhaps your company designs efficient closet space. You come into a house and design closet and shelf structures for the entire house. You have found that this makes the clients happy, but they may never be a client again unless they move into another house in your local area.

But that customer has friends and relatives and coworkers who might be potential customers for you. Word of mouth is great and effective, but give yourself a hedge by offering an incentive to your customer, such as a finder's fee or gift, for bringing in a new customer.

Part of your marketing plan should include **follow-up** calls to customers. Say you own a fencing business, and you know that fences settle after being installed. Heavy rains and winds, coupled with natural land settlement, can loosen posts and make a brand new fence appear faulty to your customer. Unless the fence completely falls down, you may or may not hear from the customer, since he may just try to reinforce the posts himself. This problem may have nothing to do with your installation techniques, but unless you've made that courtesy call and offered to go back and shore up the fence, the customer is likely to tell family and friends that you do shoddy work.

You don't need to do anything wrong to be perceived as having done something wrong. You installed the fence correctly, but you may get blamed for doing the opposite if you don't follow up properly. You not only need to sell your product, you also need to market your good name.

Mounting Your Campaign

You can find customers and clients using a variety of methods, but advertising and public relations are staples of marketing. Following are brief discussions of various types of advertising and public relations, along with examples of how they relate to freelancers.

Advertising

Television. In the age of cable television, ads are available to most businesses at a fraction of their former cost.

Locally targeted ads can be run on A&E, USA, CNN, or other national cable networks. You arrange for these ads through your area cable franchise or through your local television station. You may be able to get production help through your local television station also.

Newspapers. Statewide newspapers charge for ads by the number of people who subscribe to the paper. Whether it's cost-effective for you depends on the focus of your business. You may reach more people, but if they live 100 miles from you, and your business is giving piano lessons, there is doubt that they will become students of yours. Local weekly papers, penny savers, and the like run larger ads that will attract local clients for less money.

Magazines. If you need a way to reach a special-interest audience with your ad, many magazines offer just that. If you design plans for space-saving cabinets or art furniture, you could consider placing an ad in *Woodshop News* to reach woodworkers. If you are making your own craft items, however, and you want to sell them by mail order, you would be better off buying an ad in *Better Homes and Gardens* or a general-interest magazine that reaches a cross-section of people. Do you design crossword puzzles and word games and publish your own crossword-puzzle books? An ad in national crossword magazines could bring in business.

Radio. Radio stations cater to a particular age group. They tailor their music and ads to fit that age group. Contact the advertising salesperson at the stations that broadcast to local and statewide areas to pinpoint which station best reaches your potential customers.

Pamphlets. If your business is desktop publishing, then designing your advertisement in the form of a pamphlet is a great advertising technique. Not only will you reach possible customers, you also will be demonstrating your abilities at the same time. And unlike radio, television, and the like, when you mail your pamphlet to targeted businesses, you can make a follow-up telephone call after they've had a chance to review your work.

Flyers. If you are in the landscaping and lawn-care business, a flyer passed out in specific areas is an efficient way to reach potential customers. It's sort of a shotgun approach, though. It may not yield a high rate of return, so you need to consider how much you're willing to invest in its preparation. Like the pamphlets, you know who received the flyers, so you can canvass the neighborhood as a follow-up. Books similar to the telephone directory chronologically list street addresses, with the occupants' names and telephone numbers. One such book is the *Hill-Donnelly Cross Reference Directory*. The publisher is located in Tampa, Florida. Directories can be used as a follow-up tool if you need to call prospective customers instead of canvassing them.

Direct Mail. Do you own a carpet-cleaning business? Direct-mail services can often carry your ad for a fraction of a cent per potential customer and can usually mail to a concentrated local area. Specific towns also can be targeted with this type of advertising.

Telephone Books. Published telephone directories, such as the trademarked Yellow Pages, can be excellent sources of exposure for small businesses. You have options ranging from local telephone directories to statewide business-to-business directories. Independent companies publish phone books that contain ad sections, also. With some local telephone companies, a business telephone gets you a listing in the ad section for "free." Nothing is truly free, though. Business telephone service is more expensive than residential service.

Public Relations

Freebies. Freebies are things that your clients or customers get for free. Needless to say, you should figure in the cost of the "freebie" when you set your hourly or per job rate. Most people think of freebies as a product they can hold in their hands. As a freelancer, you have to think in more creative ways. A freebie can also be added service. If you run a pet-sitting service, part of your income may come from caring for animals on a temporary basis in people's homes. When families go away on vacation, you visit their homes a few times a day and walk, feed, and water their pets. If you're trying to land a client who takes many vacations, and you have a competitor across town who has the account now, you can "throw in" a couple of extra offerings: taking in the mail, turning lights on and off, and generally making the place look lived in while they are away. The client pays you to come in and care for the pets. The mail service, or plant-watering service, can be the freebie. You're there anyway, so the cost in time is minimal. But the service to the client is enormous.

Promotional Products and Events. You can create goodwill by giving away small items, like pens with your company name and logo on them. But you can also create goodwill by donating money to a local high-school club for use in building a float for the homecoming parade. Your company name is included on the float, and all parade viewers see you as a community-minded person. Depending on your company's scope and size, you can take the float-building idea to regional or state levels.

Seminars and Workshops. You make quilts and give lessons on quilt making for a living. Arrange to give a seminar or workshop at a local school or church. Interest people in your craft and offer a special deal to those who sign up for your classes. Maybe offer them a freebie of one free lesson if they sign up for three more.

Trade Shows and Exhibits. Every year malls sponsor exhibits on different subjects. The wedding theme is often seen year after year. As a wedding photographer/videographer, you could set up a booth with examples of your work as a great way to "advertise" yourself to your very specific type of clients. And remember, young couples who are getting married often have friends who are getting married.

Sponsorship. You are a videographer. You attend weddings, ball games, and school plays and videotape the event.

Look through your own eyes instead of the camera's for a few minutes. Take note of the names on the junior football league jerseys. By sponsoring the Video Vikings, your name is before the eyes of your potential clients. Goodwill goes a long way when a customer is choosing one company over another.

A Final Word on Communicating: Everybody Needs A Copy Editor

In the editorial world, writers often malign copy editors because copy editors get picky about such things as commas, semicolons, run-on sentences, and whether the first paragraph of a section of text should be indented. Copy editors often malign writers for not paying attention to style and grammar rules in the first place. It's a relationship of mutual respect…and sometimes one of love and hate. But if you ask any writer whether a copy editor is really necessary, the answer is usually—as it should be—"yes, definitely."

Even if you're not a writer—especially if you're not a writer—you need the equivalent of a copy editor for every piece of promotional material that goes out your door. No matter how good you think you are at catching your own typographical and grammatical errors, you need another set of eyes looking at your material with a critical glare. All you need to do is walk around a retail area and read the handwritten signs on the windows to see what can happen without that extra set of eyes:

Driver wanted

Inqire within

When you don't know how to spell *inquire,* it's better to simply write "Ask us." Don't try to be fancy if all you need is some help getting flowers delivered. Although this sign was not a promotional item, it nevertheless was seen for more than a month by all the people who passed by the florist's shop, on their way to the busy supermarket next door. A misspelled sign like that in a flower shop window might make a persnickety passerby think the shop's employees also misspell words on the cards that go out with the flowers.

What's this got to do with freelancing? You're in this alone, probably, with no one to fall back on. And you have to put your best foot forward at all times. This wouldn't be such a big deal if everyone perceived home-based businesses as just businesses. But for many potential customers, the **image** of the home comes first. Because you work from home, some people think you are less qualified or you can't get along with coworkers or you have a quirky personality.

If potential customers or clients see mistakes in your newspaper ads, bulletin board notices, newsletters, or special mailing, it only reinforces that negative image. If they see top-notch, error-free communication that shoots for and hits a target, they may just decide that it does not matter where you work. Your professionalism is what they're seeking.

Relying on computer spell checkers and grammar checkers won't suffice as a second opinion. The computer doesn't know, for instance, that you meant to say "new opportunity" rather than "news opportunity," because both are spelled correctly. Take an extra precaution and have someone else read everything you send out under the business name. You'll even find that it makes you a better writer, because you'll be on guard next time.

If you still doubt the need for an editor looking over your shoulder, pick up a *Reader's Digest* magazine and find the blurbs about typos or other "funny" errors printed in newspapers around the country. Imagine your business being the blooper in the blurb.

A Matter of Degrees

KEY TERMS

expansion   hobby
moonlighting   part-time pricing
transition   upgrade

One great thing about freelancing is that it's not an all-or-nothing proposition. It's whatever you want to make of it: occasional moonlighting, a serious part-time business, a seasonal business, a full-time business, or an expanded full-time business.

Some freelancers moonlight in their chosen profession until the moonlighting overtakes the day job. Some people start out by converting a hobby into occasional freelance jobs. Others are laid off from regular employment and turn their serious hobby into full-time freelancing, because their profession does not lend itself to immediate self-employ-

ment or regular employment. A teacher, for instance, who loses her job because of budget cutbacks, may turn to her skills as a writer and editor rather than pursue another teaching job in another town.

Freelancing also is a progressive thing. You cannot be all things to all people, and that includes yourself. As a freelancer, you have to wear many more hats than you did as someone else's employee, but you cannot wear all of them at once. Some of those hats—bookkeeper, salesperson, market analyst—may not fit properly at the beginning. The sales hat may be too loose-fitting until you shrink it down to size and make it fit your head. The today-I'm-an-expert-in-insurance hat is another one that could require several fittings.

In essence, freelancing is a matter of degrees. You have degrees of risk, financing, insurance, and expansion and degrees of accomplishment. Think of it in terms of an education. To get a master's degree, you have to earn the bachelor's degree first. There are ways to accelerate your pace, such as taking on a greater course load and not taking a summer vacation—but this comes at a price, such as mental fatigue and loss of personal time. The same is true of freelancing. You can procrastinate or take the wrong courses and never get beyond freshman status. Or you can pick the right subjects to study at the right time and sail through to the master's level.

First, decide what degree of freelancing you want to pursue:

o Make your hobby a profession

o Use your professional skills to make money on the side

o Convert your part-time business to full-time

o Launch a new full-time freelance business

o Expand or refocus your full-time freelancing business

Then, pursue your personal and business goals one degree at a time, which could mean any of the following:

o Taking a continuing-education course in accounting to speed up your understanding of it

o Raising the deductible on your health insurance to lower the premium and free up money for tools

o Establishing a line of credit at the bank to cover anticipated equipment purchases over the next six months of careful expansion

o Starting out as a sole proprietor, with the goal of incorporating within a year

o Building initial business around familiar clients, who are easier to sell to, until you are confident enough to pursue harder-to-sell but more lucrative clients

o Advertising locally at first, then expanding regionally and statewide as the income supports it

From Hobby to Profession

If you're sick of doing what you've been doing on the job for the past 10 years, or if you just retired from the military after 25 years and you want to develop a business that matches your skills and interests, you probably know that you don't want to take the first "business opportunity" that comes along. You may be a department manager in a big corporation, one that just announced it is laying off 700 workers within the next two months, and you want to switch careers so that you're never in this position again. Your motives are not entrepreneurial. Your purpose simply is to be a freelancer, and you have a marketable skill on which to base the business. Quite

DEGREES OF FREELANCING

More than Full-Time

Employment
to Self-Employment

Part-Time to Full-Time

Hobby to
Part-Time Business

often, that marketable skill is a serious **hobby.**

A hobby often has nothing to do with your occupation. An accountant may restore antique furniture on the weekend. A market analyst may be an excellent landscaper. An assembly-line foreman may be the best interior decorator within a 25-mile radius. And a librarian has traveled so often to the Orient that she could very easily become a consultant to businesses entering the export arena.

But how do you evaluate whether your hobby can be a business and, if so, decide when you should make the move? You basically follow the same procedures you would if you were taking your occupation into freelancing. You analyze your skills and compare them to potential competitors' skills, research the market you want to pursue, and decide whether you can fill a niche and be profitable at it. (See Chapter 5 for help in this phase.)

In addition to that, however, some personal considerations must be addressed before making a hobby a business:

o You may have a lot of fun with your hobby now, but if you *have* to do it to make a living, will you enjoy it?

o Do you *really* hate what you are doing professionally, or do you just need a vacation to clear your head and develop a new attitude?

o Are you using your hobby as a stopgap measure to bring in income until you can find a *real* job? If so, how seriously will you pursue the business aspect of freelancing?

The following scenarios illustrate first steps toward making a hobby a business:

o For the past 10 years, while she worked full-time as a teacher, a hobbyist potter filled her house with every imaginable kind of pottery. She also gave her relatives duplicates of many of the items found in her home. If she continues turning out work at her current pace, she could have several boxes of handmade vessels stacked up next to and on top of an idle kiln. It's time to sign up for a craft show and sell some of those pieces.

o A librarian has just returned from her eighth trip to Japan. On the return flight, she met a businessman who had been trying to arrange a deal for his company to export an agricultural product to Japan. He couldn't discuss the nature of the product with her; he operates in a highly competitive environment, and he wanted to seal the deal before another company did. The librarian offered to do some research for the businessman when she got back home. He accepted and offered to pay her handsomely for a written report based on her research and her special knowledge of Japanese culture. While the librarian does research for this businessman, perhaps she can discover other companies that may need her specialized services.

The teacher and librarian know that they have marketable skills that can be turned into businesses. They know that they are competent enough at those skills to survive in the freelancing world. By exhibiting at craft shows, the teacher will learn quickly the potential for sales and income from pottery. The librarian will also reach a fairly quick conclusion that a definite commercial need exists for her unique experience and knowledge. Now comes the hard part.

Will the teacher miss seeing 25 eager faces as she explains the mysteries of math to a bunch of sixth graders? Will she be able to work alone all the time after being involved in such a people-oriented profession? The answer may be an unqualified "go for it," because she has reached a different plateau in life or because the neighborhood in which she teaches just isn't safe to drive through any more, even in the daytime. She also is tired of teacher's jobs being the sacrificial lambs that school boards offer up every year to quiet taxpayers' opposition to the school budget.

Will the librarian miss the library? Will she miss the security of knowing that when she comes back from a trip to Hokkaido, she has a steady paycheck to help pay for the trip? Will her travels be as much fun when she has a much stricter schedule and budget to meet in business than when she traveled on her own agenda and itinerary? Or is she ready to capitalize on her own inner strengths and the cultural expertise she has worked so hard to develop?

Turning a hobby into a business involves a higher degree of personal evaluation than is required when turning your existing occupation into freelancing. Doing it can turn out to be the best decision you ever made—or the most dangerous. Try not to let the personal decisions get clouded with dreams and fantasies that override common-sense business matters.

If You Just Want To Moonlight

Moonlighting means taking occasional jobs on the side or working part-time on a steady basis. It is common in many occupations, with people who want to make extra money for a specific purpose, or with others who want to test their skills at freelancing while still tethered to the corporation and its benefits. Moonlighting is done by people who have the full consent of their employers, and it's done under the cloak of secrecy.

Managing the moonlighting takes a special knack. But if you're good at it, you probably will be a good freelancer. You have to be able to balance the demands of the extra work with the demands of your regular job and your family. It's easy to get caught up in a situation that robs you of sleep, patience, your alertness at work, and your tolerance of family members. When you get to the point where this is happening all the time, you have to give up something, either the moonlighting or the day job.

The advantages of moonlighting before you plunge full-time into freelancing center around management and finances. Trying something on an occasional or part-time basis lowers your risk considerably, while you develop those sales skills or while you design a home-office plan that works for you and does not interfere too much with the teenagers in the house. You also may be able to put everything you make moonlighting back into the business, because your salary is meeting all your financial needs right now. Doing so can give you a better financial footing when you do want to launch a full-time effort. One temptation to steer away from is learning to depend on or enjoy the moonlighting income for regular or entertainment expenses. The financial demands of this new life-style will make switching to full-time freelancing more difficult.

From Part-Time To Full-Time

If you've been moonlighting as a small-business accountant while working full-time at a huge international accounting firm, and you like the personal contact in small business better than the impersonal trans-Atlantic faxes, then your decision to go full-time into freelancing probably is already made. It's just a matter of when. It's time to ask existing accounts if they know of other small businesses who can use your services. Then draw up a projection as to what it will cost to leave the firm.

But maybe you are a part-time wedding photographer, who has reached the point where you need more equipment.

The above accountant would say you cannot justify the purchase of additional equipment if you do not have more jobs lined up. It's time to buy an ad in the local paper, have a new brochure printed, and check on whether the darkroom can be expanded to take on full-time volume. If the promotion is successful, you'll have enough new customers to quit working as a corporate photographer.

Even if you are a part-time freelancer, you still need to concentrate on making a profit from your business. This will not only train you to think in the proper direction, it will help you finance the venture you want to pursue. If the above photographer priced his work to earn a profit as a part-timer, he would have enough money to purchase the new equipment. The question then becomes, "will the market pay him back?"

One common pitfall in part-time freelancing is to price your work according to part-time or short-term goals. In other words, you charge for your services according to **part-time pricing.** You get more work that way, possibly, but you make a lot less money. And you make it rough on yourself when you have to explain to steady customers why you raised prices for the same service just because you went from part-time to full-time.

Some common considerations when thinking of going from part-time to full-time are whether your present equipment and space are capable of full-time use, whether you need to borrow money to finance the expansion, and whether you are up to the task of running a full-time business.

Cutting the Ties: From Employed To Self-employed

Making the shift from employed to self-employed amounts to first-degree freelancing. Every chapter in this book contains information on different aspects of this. So here, an effort is made to list more of the endless details that go along with the **transition.** You accomplish this move best by looking at the big picture, while still focusing on the close-up angles.

Financing

If you are self-financing your enterprise—and many freelancers start out this way—implementing certain money management techniques before you leave your employment can help. These include

o Consolidating personal debts into one lower-interest account.

o Refinancing your home at a lower interest rate.

o Researching local banks to determine which is friendliest to small businesses. What are monthly fee amounts? Does the bank have interest-bearing accounts for businesses?

One of the best ways to help finance a new venture is to take part of your old job with you. Many freelancers end up working for former employers, just on a different level. If you can work out a retainer type of arrangement, or a specific contract, you can usually consider it money in the bank.

If you are seeking financing for your business, it takes more planning and research. You will need a business plan (see Chapter 13), and you'll have to prove that your market research is solid.

Sources of financing include:

o Your own home, if you can arrange for a home-equity loan before you leave your employment

o Your relatives, although this can get sticky if you lose the money

o Your local bank, either through a personal line of credit or a business start-up loan

o The Small Business Administration, possibly a guaranteed loan through a bank

o Your own corporation, if you are sophisticated enough and have the proper legal and financial setup to raise capital by selling stock

Image

First impressions are critical in business. Looking professional will go a long way toward establishing business credibility. Think carefully, and seek professional advice if possible, on what type of promotional materials you will need. And make sure they are designed and produced with your goals in mind. For instance, if your business will depend on a small base of clients, you might put more effort and money into a comprehensive, impressive promotional folder containing your business card, a brochure on your background and your

services, and a list of references. If you're going to be pursuing many customers, however, you could consider spending that same money on a splashy print-ad campaign and getting less-expensive brochures.

But the professional image comes from more than just printed matter. A resume and portfolio may have been enough to get you another job, but this isn't just another job. It's your life.

Think of your image as a whole-business concept. Not only do you perform your work well, on time, and with a pleasant attitude, but you also handle your business affairs with equal ability. The image is more than just appropriate stationery and a color brochure. It's also a perception among your suppliers, your bank, clients, and potential clients that you manage your time well, pay your bills on time, and still have some time left over for the family and the community.

In freelancing, you need to make a positive first impression, then keep building on that through your everyday work.

Expanding an Existing Freelancing Business

Even if you are just now making the break from employment to freelancing, you need to think about **expansion.** How big do you want to get? Businesses tend to operate in cycles. First, you have tremendous growth in the beginning stages. Starting from one small contract, it's easy to have a 100 percent increase in sales in a short period of time. Then the growth levels off, and you reach a plateau. If you managed your cash flow and made a profit during the initial stages, you'll be better able to settle down and take a hard look at your business when growth subsides and routine takes over. While some businesses seem to exist forever at this plateau, others either enter another growth phase or fall because of complacency and poor planning.

Take some time periodically to analyze what you are doing now and compare that to what you want to be doing a year from now. You can even keep a running list of such goals to track incremental progress. And expansion doesn't necessarily mean you have to give up your home base of operation. Expansion can mean just working smarter and making more money in the same space.

From your existing home-based business, you can expand by

o Hiring an employee

o Subcontracting work to other free-lancers

o Getting new and higher-paying clients

o Forming a consortium, or joint venture, with other freelancers

o Taking on a partner

o Contracting out to others some of the time-consuming business tasks such as bookkeeping

o Hiring a sales representative, so you can spend more time working at your own profession

Some practical considerations when deciding on expansion include assessing your present equipment status and pro-jecting future needs. You may be able to get a bigger contract by offering to do more work, but do you have the necessary tools and equipment? Is your computer up to the job?

If you're a writer with a flair for publication design also, you may want to get a bigger piece of the pie by offering to write and produce a client's brochure. But writing only requires that you have a word-processing program and possibly an ink-jet printer. Page layout and production will necessitate more software and a laser printer. You may have to use every dime from that first job just to replenish the cash flow from having to buy the new products. But once you've expanded your setup, you're ready for the next profitable job.

One consideration with computers and software is whether you'll have to **upgrade** or buy new hardware just to be able to run an advanced software program. Even newer word-processing programs can be awfully sluggish if your computer only has enough memory to run the previous version of the program. Just as you have to think of your image in whole-business terms, you have to think of your computer needs in whole-system terms.

Switching from being a sole proprietor to a corporation is another degree of expansion. When you went into business, you didn't have time to handle all the paperwork required by a corporate structure. You decided to keep things as simple as possible and remain a sole proprietor. But if you have reached a more complicated stage in business, it may be beneficial to incorporate, particularly if the complications expose you to financial liability and more taxes. Maybe now you have one employee, and you have the money to hire a bookkeeper to come in once a week. Maybe a sales representative is bringing in new business.

With the exception of the subchapter S corporation, if that option is available in your state, corporations have to pay corporate income tax, then the corporation's employees—you, in this case—have to pay personal income taxes on salary and wages. There are ways to adjust what you take out of the company as personal income to balance the tax differences, but this takes a steady hand at managing the corporation while you also do your main work—or else you have to hire a good bookkeeper and accountant. One advantage to running your own corporation is that you can set the corporation's fiscal year to end on a different schedule than the calendar, which allows you more personal tax flexibility.

Other corporate versus proprietorship considerations include the following:

o Corporations have to deduct payroll taxes and pay workers' compensation insurance on all employees, even if the owner is the only employee. The payroll should also be a formally arranged matter and a matter of meticulous bookkeeping. As a sole proprietor, you can take a "draw" whenever you need it for personal reasons, keep track of it more easily, then pay estimated taxes quarterly based on your net income.

o Corporations can pay for their employees' health insurance, whereas sole proprietors can only deduct 25 percent of the premium.

o Corporate tax returns are more complicated, and therefore more expensive, to fill out than proprietorship or partnership returns.

o Dissolving a corporation, if it doesn't work out, requires more paperwork than dissolving a proprietorship and usually a partnership, depending on the partnership's complexity.

CHAPTER THIRTEEN

A Road Map: How Do You Get There from Here?

KEY TERMS

business plan

insurance

profit-and-loss statement

buying in bulk

listening

retirement

When you travel, it is often better to know where *not* to go and what route not to take. The same can be said for the freelancing business. Just as a visitor to town needs to know which streets to avoid during rush hour, so he can get to the airport on time, a freelancer needs to study the mistakes others have made and try to skirt around them.

It is easy to dismiss other people's mistakes by saying, "Oh, I wouldn't do *that*" or "Yeah, right! I wouldn't be *that* stupid." Then, two months after you're in business, you realize you forgot to order another print run of your brochure, and you just handed the last one out yesterday. Too bad you have an important sales presentation at 2:00 P.M., and not a brochure in sight. By the way, where did you leave those new, specially designed, expensive presentation folders you brought home yesterday?

Just hope that a brochure printing is the only thing you're "not stupid enough" to forget when you have too many entries on the daily calendar. Other mistakes can be disastrous, such as missing a delivery for a client, not being able to deposit the client's check, and not having enough cash on hand to cover the checks you've written because you were counting on that income today.

A full range of concepts, ideas, and methods used in freelancing has been discussed in other chapters of this book. In this chapter, methods and tips on how to bring it all together are offered—but first, a look at what *not* to do.

Common Mistakes

First, the Mistakes...

The reason you will see a similar list of common business mistakes in most books about business is this: Everybody keeps making them. People still think they can turn their hobby into a business just because they do their hobby very well. People still think that even though there isn't enough money in the bank for one month, let alone six, that magic event will take place and hordes of clients will sign up the first day after they quit their day jobs. That may happen. But what if it doesn't? Do you have a backup?

Common causes of failure for free-lancers relate to both internal and external factors and to various aspects of business and personality. You can be an expert at what you do, but a real amateur at selling. You can sell all day long, but if you can't schedule a delivery or if you don't have a legitimate product or service, it's to no avail. Following is a list of the deadliest sins for freelancers:

o Lack of management
o Lack of vision
o Insufficient funds to start and run a business
o Overdependence on too few people, mainly yourself
o Poor marketing and selling
o Poor communication, internal and external
o Lack of money management
o Too much technical concentration, not enough attention to business
o Inability to analyze needs and wishes of clients/customers
o Underestimating competition, overestimating ability to deal with it
o Erosion of self-confidence
o Poor service/products
o Lack of support from other people, businesses
o Poor record keeping
o Lack of interpersonal skills
o Inability to assess personal skills
o Refusal to consider criticism or accept responsibility
o Lack of planning
o Undedicated or unscrupulous partners
o Too much work and not enough play
o Inability to cope with stress
o Procrastination
o Lack of flexibility
o Failure to keep up with trends—business, technology, etc.

Then, Some Preventive Medicine

Some things you can do to avoid the above mistakes:

o Have a plan and go by it
o See a lawyer and an accountant
o Respect the tax laws

o Learn and abide by the town laws

o Build and maintain your network of associates and friends

o Don't procrastinate

o Listen to your customers/clients

o Either learn financial planning or pay someone to do it for you

o Maintain and expand your expertise at your occupation

o Recognize your limitations

o Accept responsibility

o Be innovative

o Think about the future and what you want it to bring

Get a Plan

If you could take all the other chapters in this book and fold them into one, it would manifest itself as a **business plan.** So why a business plan? After all, it's just you in that small extra bedroom working on your computer...or in the garage making wooden toys...or in the kitchen baking muffins. You need a business plan for several reasons, but the most important one is for the same reason you need a road map if you're traveling in unfamiliar territory. Basically, you can't get there from here without a map.

No matter what type of freelancer you are—traditional, transitional, or reluctant—a business blueprint can help you achieve success. After all, freelancing is a big-enough gamble on its own merit, so why not hedge your bet with at least a bit of business planning? It does not have to be elaborate. It just needs to fit your needs, and you can develop it by asking yourself questions, then research-ing and finding out the answers. You may have already developed this plan as a result of what your read in Chapter 7.

Write your plan in plain, everyday language. You can revise it as necessary, and you can expand it according to your growth. If you later use it to seek a bank loan, you need to have someone else read it over and offer some criticism. And if you get so busy you have to formalize it, consult one of the many books available on business plans, including *The Perfect Business Plan Made Simple* by William Lasher, Ph.D., CPA, published by Doubleday in 1994.

Start by writing an outline, then filling in the details:

I. The Business: Its Scope and Purpose

II. The Market: Its Size and Characteristics

III. Equipment and Physical Requirements

IV. Management and Staffing

V. Financial Requirements and Projections

> **Business Planning**

The Business: Its Scope and Purpose

The first question you need to answer is, "What will I do to make a living?" If you're like most freelancers, the answer is easy: The same thing you've been doing as someone else's employee.

You're good at it, you know people in the business, and you can make a go of it on your own. Your purpose is to offer a good service for a fair price, while making yourself a better personal and professional life.

Others have a hobby or skill that is a potential money-maker. Joanie makes specialty cakes. She makes turkey-shaped cakes at Thanksgiving and Raggedy Ann and Andy cakes for her friends' children's birthdays. Word of mouth has friends of friends calling her and asking what she would charge for this or that kind of cake. No bakery in town makes cakes like Joanie's. Sitting on a gold mine, Joanie decided to go into freelancing and make cakes in her kitchen; no one was surprised.

But not all potential freelancers have such defined careers, and they have to look around the community and fit their skills to what is needed commercially. Your particular situation will partly determine what you do. Beverly, a mother with three preschoolers, decides to work at a home-based business because she'd need to work as a brain surgeon to make enough money to pay for her three young ones to attend a day-care center. Starting up an errand-running business for shut-ins is probably not her best business choice, because she'd still be out of the house and still need some sort of day care for her children. But since she used to be a public relations director for a company that ran four area nursing homes, she can take a night-school computer course to bring her desktop publishing skills up to date. Perhaps her former employer needs newsletters written and produced, a job she can handle without leaving the house.

The Market: Its Size And Characteristics

Just like Joanie with her cakes, you want a business that is welcome in your town. Don't start baking in your kitchen if there are other good bakeries in town. Don't open a management consulting business without first checking how many similar businesses are also in the vicinity.

While some freelancers—writers, for instance—can live just about anywhere, others will need to hone their skills to fit the needs of their location. If your location doesn't suit you, maybe you can operate long-distance if your occupation allows you to do that. Many freelancers have few local clients.

Size up your competitors and the potential for clients/customers. When you start writing all of this information down in your business plan, it soon becomes obvious where the holes are that need to be filled in.

Within this section, you also need a marketing plan, as was developed in Chapter 11.

Equipment and Physical Requirements

Use the lists you developed in Chapter 8 as your basic requirements for tools, computers, and space alterations. Be sure to include any transportation requirements the business has and describe how they will be met.

Management and Staffing

This most likely will just be your resume to start. But include any plans you have for hiring part-time help, getting help from your spouse when you need it, or any subcontracting arrangements you have worked out.

Financial Requirements And Projections

Include your start-up budget, your operating budget, and projections of sales and expenses for the first year. List the sources of your funding and any plans to seek financing from lenders. Also, include how you will price your products/services, how your pricing compares to competitors' pricing, and how and when it will net you a profit. You also need to write a section that describes how finances will be handled if your sales do not meet projections.

Working Within the Plan To Meet Day-to-Day Requirements

A completed business plan, as a component of your overall personal and professional goals, becomes a cornerstone in your foundation for success. But it is not something you will consult 50 times a day to decide how to do something. Those decisions come from within yourself, based on your knowledge, experience, and consultations with people in your network. The remainder of this chapter offers various suggestions that may prove to be signposts along the route to successful freelancing.

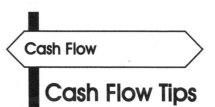

Cash Flow

Cash Flow Tips

You read how to project cash flow at the end of Chapter 10. But managing cash flow is an ongoing proposition. It involves not only how you spend money, but how you take it in.

o Keeping a regular running account of your current jobs or sales will help. List the dates of the sales, the dates of amounts due, and the phone number to call if bills due are not in on time.

o Most people and companies get a lot of bills around the first of the month. If you bill on a monthly basis, send your bills out at the end of the month, so they are at the front of the line when they reach their destination. This isn't a guarantee that you'll get paid first, but it does prevent the client from forgetting you.

o One way to encourage early or prompt payments is to offer a 1 percent or 2 percent discount if the bill is paid by the tenth of the month. Many businesses will take advantage of this. Look at this from your accounts payable perspective, also. You can make up any discount a client takes by paying your own bills on time and getting a discount from someone else.

○ Specify on the invoice what the late fee is if the bill is paid after a certain date—and be firm in collecting it. Uncollected money costs you more.

○ If a bill is a few days late, place a phone call to the account. Be helpful at first, and the money may come immediately. Clients who are having cash flow problems may pay the people who are nicest to them first. Then again, the check may really have gotten lost in the mail, and if you're not nice, you may not get another chance.

○ If you get a big check this month, and you see you don't need it all until four months down the road, put it in a short-term investment.

Taxes and Accounting

Tax-Savings Tips

Do not file your income taxes based solely on the tips you read about in magazines, newspapers, and business books. Taxes are as personal as taste in food, and a lot more dangerous. Don't get blindsided by a deduction you read about somewhere and took that comes back as disallowed by the Internal Revenue Service, along with a "balance due" note instead of a refund check. If you fill out your own taxes, it is best to get a certified public accountant to review them before you file. You can buy

computer software for both personal and business taxes that helps you through the myriad of forms and also alerts you to certain "red flags" you have listed in your return. The IRS has a number of points that it uses to identify potential returns for audit, and the home-office deduction is one of those red flags. So your figures must be entered and checked carefully.

Keeping that in mind, you might consider some of the following tax-savings tips:

○ If you have a big contract that has a scheduled payment due just before the end of the year, look carefully at what that income is going to do to your taxes. If it will save you tax money by delaying the income a few days into the next year, you can either ask the client to withhold payment a few days, or if the client needs to make the payment to improve his tax situation, just don't open your mail until the first of the year. You can't deposit a check you don't know you have.

○ Take the most effective route when deciding whether to depreciate a new piece of equipment or expense it out in one year. That option has been improved over the past two years.

○ If possible, time your payment of local and state taxes to help reduce your federal taxes. If you have local or state taxes due the first month of the year, try paying them a month early to reduce your federal tax amount.

○ On loans where the interest is deductible by the business, which can included a portion of your mort-

---

BEFORE YOU BEGIN WORK

ON A LONG-TERM PROJECT, ...

(Negotiate Contract)

(Have Contract Reviewed by Attorney)

Getting a deposit up front helps with cash flow and adds security to a project.

(Sign Contract)

(Get Deposit)

(Start Work)

---

gage if you take the home-office deduction, make your January payment in December. That will increase the interest deduction to the degree of interest you had accrued through the end of the year.

Don't Nickel-and-Dime Yourself Into Bankruptcy

When setting up your home office or shop, what part is the most fun? For many, it's the chance to buy all these new gadgets and supplies. A trip to the office-supply superstore or the membership warehouse can allow you to get everything you need in one trip. Or if you're in a rural area, you may like thumbing through catalogs and making choices. After you are in business, however, buying for the business becomes a chore that requires as much attention to detail as your bookkeeping. Let yourself have some fun in the beginning, as long as you don't go overboard, but step back

and watch what you're doing after the business is up and running.

All home-office supplies are tax-deductible. And the amount of otherwise depreciable equipment you can expense directly in one year has increased recently, to $17,000 on 1993 federal returns. This makes it highly advantageous to plan your equipment and supplies purchases by tax year. Just make sure you are buying for the business and not the home.

When buying office supplies, consider **buying in bulk.** If you have a place to store 10 cases of copy paper, which you use in both the copy machine and the laser printer, you can get a break from most suppliers. A number of mail-order office supply dealers use copy paper as one of their prime products to advertise, so it's easy to compare prices.

Also, plan your office needs, and when you have to go for one thing, try and anticipate something else you may need. One trip to get a number of items, or one mail-order shipping charge for a consolidated shipment, will save you many dollars over the long term. But if you buy supplies one ballpoint pen and one legal pad at a time, you'll find that the nickels and dimes you wasted total up to a stack worth dollars and dollars.

Get Money Up Front

If you provide a service to clients or you build expensive items that take several weeks to make, get a deposit up front. It is common practice and a safer way of doing business. For instance, if you are a computer consultant, and a small business wants you to design a custom computer system, including buying the hardware and software, then installing it on their premises, use their money for all of your initial expenses and time. It is not unusual to ask for a 50 percent deposit before starting to work. That way, your liability is covered in case the other business burns down before you can complete your work.

After the deposit, you can schedule an interim payment based on a percentage of completion or future date, then get the final payment when you deliver the product. This type of arrangement not only lessens your risk if something disastrous happens to the other business, it protects you if the other business owner is just a jerk who likes to take advantage of people. If you have suspicions of the latter, however, make sure your contract is clear about what happens to the deposit if the work is canceled midstream.

Insurance

Insurance and The Freelancer

Paying for **insurance**, particularly health insurance, is a major disadvantage in freelancing. Health-care costs have skyrocketed for a variety of reasons. Why is not important. What is important is that they have, and as a freelancer, you have to deal with it. Options available to the freelancer are discussed below.

Spousal Insurance

If your spouse is employed by a mega corporation or a business that offers health insurance as one of the fringe benefits, then your coverage can be included in that. Company-sponsored insurance is almost always less expensive than an individually purchased plan.

Buying into Your Existing Plan

If you are leaving a company with an insurance plan, you can take that plan with you for 18 months. It's usually not cheap, because you will have to pay all of the premiums, but if you or your spouse is pregnant, or if some other sort of continual care condition exists, it may not be covered if you change plans.

Shopping Around

Buying health insurance nowadays is even more complicated than buying a car. You can see the cars, test-drive them, read consumer reports, and get a fairly good idea of what you are getting for your money. You've owned cars before—basically, you know what to look for when buying. There is even a "lemon law" that protects you, the consumer, if the car does not perform as advertised. But when you buy health insurance, it may be your first time buying. What is and is not paid for by the insurance companies varies greatly from company to company, and the details can get very confusing.

Insurance policies now come in many different styles with many different services. If the person you will be insuring—you, a spouse, or child—has an illness that requires years of continual care, then your needs are different than the ones that will be discussed here. In this case, you will need to know the fine points of each policy available and will need to seek the services of a professional independent insurance agent.

Regardless of your age, the physical condition of you and your family, and your family's needs, an independent agent is the place to start, since she has access to many companies, large and small.

The deductible, the out-of pocket expenses you are required to pay before the insurance company starts to pay a medical bill, varies greatly. You can find policies with deductibles ranging from $0 to $10,000. And these policies have a range in price tags (premiums) that is just as great.

HMOs, or health maintenance organizations, are available, but the cost for a family plan can be substantial, easily twice the cost of a basic high-deductible policy. HMOs, however, cover nearly 100 percent of your medical care for all types of medical needs, ranging from maternity, well-visits, and major surgery.

Some professional organizations have a group plan that can be joined, and some state business associations also have access to a plan that has open enrollment. Start with the chamber of commerce in your state, as each state has different plans. Some states allow freelancers—since freelancers are businesses with at least 1 employee—and small businesses with 25 employees or less to become part of plans that are available to very large corporations. By joining the local business associations and the chamber of commerce, you can keep abreast of what changes are taking place in the insurance industry.

Disability Insurance

Disability insurance, or insurance that pays you if you cannot work, is very expensive. Policies run $1,500 a year or more and are difficult to collect on (because it is hard for you to prove that you are not working at home when your business is at home) and rarely pay enough to support your life-style. They also are outrageously expensive if your type of work is the slightest bit dangerous, such as framing houses. Saving the $1,500 or more in a high-yield account might pay in the long run. One possibility is placing the money that would have gone to a disability plan into an Individual Retirement Account (see below for a more detailed explanation).

Life Insurance

If you worked for the mega corporation, you most likely would have had some sort of term life insurance that, if nothing else, would probably have been enough to bury you. As a freelancer, even a freelancer whose spouse works for the mega corporation, you may have nothing—unless you take the option to pay the premiums and convert the former company life insurance to your own name. You probably can find more attractive premiums on your own, however.

Life insurance becomes more expensive with age, but it is not that expensive to the young nonsmoking, healthy freelancer just starting out. There are certain things a freelancer should consider when buying life insurance.

Your age and net worth. If you are near retirement age, your kids are through school, your house is paid for, your bank account is well padded, and the company downsizes you right out the door, life insurance probably isn't worth the cost. But if you've just started a freelancing business and your family is young, then a visit to an independent agent is essential. In most cases, if you die, so does your business.

Company value with or without you. If your business is a partnership, possibly a husband-and-wife writing team, then you will need to have enough insurance to replace your salary—unless your spouse will be able to write twice as fast once you're gone. Otherwise, your spouse suddenly has to support the family on half of the normal income.

Family and dependents. If you think that losing your job due to downsizing was traumatic for your family, imagine dying without leaving them a "salary" in the form of life insurance. A good independent agent can figure out your needs and what type of insurance gives you the most for your money.

Homeowner's Insurance

Your homeowner's insurance may or may not cover your working out of your house. You should check with your agent as to whether the policy covers business equipment and liability if either customers come to your home or employees work in your home. There is no substitute for talking to your agent about what is and is not covered by your present policy.

> Retirement Planning

Retirement Planning

One of the fringe benefits that comes with working for the mega corporation is a **retirement** or pension plan. Unless you want to be working and/or living on Social Security after 65—some would say that's a bigger gamble than freelancing—you'd better start planning ahead. If you worked for the mega corporation for a certain period of time, you are "vested." This means that you are part of their retirement and/or pension plans and that money in your name is yours to keep when you leave the company. If you put it directly into an IRA in a bank, it will not be considered income and will not be taxed. Otherwise, you may owe a lot to Uncle Sam. Many different types of plans are available to the freelancer:

IRA

Advantages. This is an individual retirement account that can be contributed to by both employed and self-employed individuals. Up to $2,000 can be put into an IRA each year. Self-employed people also can contribute to a Keogh Plan (see below). You have until April 15, or whatever your filing date, not including extensions, to make the contribution for the previous tax year. These funds are available without early withdrawal penalty if you become disabled, so it can be considered a type of disability insurance. Otherwise, you can withdraw the funds after the age of 59½. IRA contributions need not be the same each year, and some years can even be skipped if the "lean-year monster" gets you from time to time. After 59½, the funds can either be fully withdrawn, and taxed, or withdrawn in installments at a lower tax rate than if the full amount were withdrawn.

Disadvantages. The IRA is limited to $2,000 per year, which means that you'd better start saving early for it to amount to anything for retirement.

SEP IRA

Advantages. This is a simplified employee-pension individual-retirement account and is a great type of plan if you have just a few employees. The account usually is set up through a bank, but it can also be set up through an insurance company that is involved with multiple investment options. All employees, including yourself, could be included. All would receive the same percentage amount in their accounts, up to 15 percent of their earnings or $30,000, whichever is higher.

Disadvantages. You must include all employees who have worked for you for at least three of the last five years and are over the age of 21. Employees can withdraw from the account (there are penalties), and you have no say in the matter.

SRF

A salary reduction IRA is one in which you and your employees decide how much of your salaries to put away. Only half of your employees need to participate.

Keogh Plan

Advantages. This type of plan allows the self-employed person to put more money away each year—either $30,000 or 25 percent of salary, whichever is less. The plan needs to exist before the last day of the year, and the money needs to be in the account by the company's tax-filing date.

THE SEARCH FOR GOOD SERVICE NEVER ENDS

A long time ago, in the early 1980s, I lived on an island off Georgia's coast. It had a population of 10,000, was just off the coast of a town with a population of 25,000, in a county with a population of 50,000.

At the time, my hair was cut short in a Dorothy Hamill sort of cut, which meant visiting the hairdresser every six weeks to keep the style in shape.

I had a wonderful hairdresser, although I was not appreciative of her wondrous abilities, since I previously wore my hair long and had not had to contend with the haircut ritual every six weeks or so. She listened to me, answered my questions, and told me things about my hair—what type of hair I had, which styles would or would not do well on me.

After marrying, I moved with my family to "bigger and better" cities and states. My hair, of course, waited not for time and still needed that six-week cut. (Actually, my hair grows faster than the average and needs to be cut every four weeks, another tidbit I learned from the previous hairdresser.)

Unfortunately, what followed after I left the island was a series of disappointments that continue to haunt me today. My next few hairdressers at salons—ranging from the "quick-cut walk-ins welcome" place to the pooh-pooh salons with fancy furnishings and classical music playing—all had the same attitude. They didn't want to hear about my hair or what difficulties I had had in the past. Snip, snip, snip, and I was out the door. I'd go home and admonish myself for not being more assertive. After all, I was the customer. Wasn't I supposed to be treated better? Weren't they supposed to listen to me?

When my hair started to gray in my early 30s, I made the rounds to the different salons trying to find one that would treat me with some sort of respect. If you think

Disadvantage. If you employ anyone, you might also have to set up a Keogh plan for them, too.

Never Stop Listening

Sometimes, your profit or loss factor may be in the way you treat your clients and customers. You continually have to look at yourself through your client's eyes.

Are you giving them what they want and when they want it?

Do you know what they want?

Take a moment to consider one or two individuals who deal with you regularly.

Can you recite the last two requests they made of you?

What about the client you haven't seen in six months?

Did she move away or was she unhappy with you when you had a bad day?

you feel stupid when you go to the doctor's office, try going to the hairdresser's. With your head in the sink, the only thing you are asked is, "What are you using to shampoo your hair?" I swear, there is no right answer unless it is sold in the salon.

With each new salon, I would tell the hairdresser the horror story of the last place. At one salon, the hairdresser "forgot" in what style I wore my hair, and before I could stop her, my hair was cut in a pixie. I looked like an over-the-hill Tinkerbell! When I "freaked out," her only response was, "Oh, don't worry. It'll grow back."

Again, I looked for a new hairdresser. I once remarked to my new stylist that a telephone call to a customer who had not been back for her six-week color and cut might bring back a potentially disgruntled customer. When I left her, she never called.

Today, my hairdresser colors my hair—I think, too light—and she calls me "Meggie." My name is "Mickey." I corrected her once. My hair needs to be cut and colored every four weeks, and the appointment card always is for six weeks later. I asked her to please make it every four. If this were my doctor, and every time he gave me a prescription it was for a medicine to which I was allergic, I'd find a new doctor. But I say nothing. My experience is that it doesn't do any good with a lot of hairdressers. I'm about to resign myself to poor service and give up looking. Then, I think about the future.

My husband and I are now planning for our retirement. And one of our top choices is the island where we met and married, which he thinks is my reason for wanting to return. But I know a great hairdresser there who listens!

— Margaret "Mickey" Hand

To get a personal account of the effect of **listening**—or not listening—see the box above.

Set Up a Record-keeping System You Will Use

You can pay the most expensive CPA in New York City to develop your bookkeeping and accounting system if you want. But if you don't understand how to use it—worse yet, if you just don't use it at all—it does no one but that accountant any good. Just remember to keep track of every cup of coffee you buy for your clients and every paper clip you buy for the office. Write down your mileage on the car, and separate the personal and business miles.

A simple bookkeeping system could be two shoe boxes under your desk, one marked "Money In" and one marked "Money Out." You put receipts, deposit slips, invoices, whatever, in the appropriate box. You could then hire a professional bookkeeper to come in once a week, sort it all out, and keep your records up-to-date. But the more you know about bookkeeping, such as how to compile and read a **profit-and-loss statement** and how to read a potential client's financial statement, the better you will be at running a business.

Keeping a journal is a start. You give every transaction its own line in chronological order. Then you progress to a ledger, where you can enter transactions first according to whether they are income or expenses, then according to the types of expenses, such as advertising or utilities.

After that, develop your own profit-and-loss statement, plus an assets-and-liabilities statement. You can do all of this using traditional pencil and paper or by purchasing a simple bookkeeping software package for your computer.

Whether you make a profit or you chalk up a loss, use your records to see how you can improve your business. Make your own analysis, and then seek help whenever you need it.

PART SIX

WHY DO YOU FREELANCE?

CHAPTER FOURTEEN

Motivating Factors

KEY TERMS

automation   *global economy*
growth   *trust*

Why should you freelance? It's an extremely personal question that only you can answer for yourself. If you want to pursue a "dream," how anchored is that dream to the reality of business? If you just lost your job at a corporation, can freelancing provide a long-term method of achieving your lifetime goals, or just a short-term way to put food on the table? The process of deciding why you should freelance is integrated into every phase of the decision on whether you should freelance. It involves all of the variables: what, who, when, where, and how.

Perhaps what you do and how you do it does not conform to mass-production or big-corporation standards and methods, and you can only do what you want to do if you're self-employed. Maybe you advise small businesses on tax matters and financial planning. Can you recommend various options better as a member of a corporate staff or as an equal of the small business owner? If it doesn't matter to you which way you do it, then it's probably advisable to remain a member of the corporate staff. You may not have the motivation to succeed as a freelancer. But if you think the corporation tends to recommend one or more specific options most often because of tradition or outright prejudice and not because of new research, then that may be why you want to be your own boss.

If you've spent 15 years developing your professional engineering abilities, making contacts in the field and generally making a good life for yourself and your family, do you want to trust the big company you've been working for to continue to offer you the same sense of security and prosperity? Many people can. But in other cases, any evidence of job security is difficult to detect. As the world gets smaller economically and closer together because of technology, the face of traditional employment is changing. Some jobs that used to be in Tennessee are now in Mexico. Some jobs do not exist in Massachusetts any more because the market went south, then to Thailand. And some high-tech jobs that Californians thought were permanent are now in Arizona—or India.

Maybe you've had your fill of high tech. You personally saw computers go from the monster-sized metal cages that filled the back rooms of businesses to the tiny notebooks that can fit in a briefcase. You know what computers are capable of doing, and you respect people's abilities to increase productivity by using computers. But what you like better is working with your hands, perhaps building an old-fashioned rolltop desk or creating attractive landscaping environments in residential suburbs and commercial business parks. You've decided you want more out of life than sheer "productivity." If it takes an extra half-hour to place a series of plants in such a way that they make a homesite look warm and welcome, then it's your time and you can do it. You don't have to

worry about the day's efficiency factor, because you'll trust yourself to make it up another day.

...left a good job in the city...

One reason why people risk everything and start their own freelancing business at home is because, basically, life is too short.

A man who wanted nothing more than to work in publishing moved from the South to Connecticut and took a position with a national publication. When he outgrew this job, each week he would buy the Sunday *New York Times,* read the employment section, and send out resumes in search of a job in New York City. Finally, the job offer came. It was a great job, on paper. Oh yes, he was assured, he'd be able to move up. And he could count on catching the 5:35 p.m. train back to Connecticut, so he could still have some semblance of family life. This man was married and had two teenage daughters, who were growing up faster than fathers want their little girls to grow up. Soon, they'd be going to college.

The job was more political than substantive. Soon, the man realized why this position was open. Soon, he realized that this job, and a million more at this level, meant giving up a family life at least five, and sometimes six, days a week. "Politics" meant putting in some hours just so the boss would see you there with him, 90 minutes after the 5:35 Metro North express pulled out of Grand Central Terminal.

So the man left the "prestigious" position in New York City. He started his own freelancing business out of his home in Connecticut. He writes books and makes more money than he did in the City. And he sees his teenage daughters and his wife everyday.

But maybe you have a different motive. Maybe you have a necessity to freelance.

Yes, Do Try This at Home

Automation. Feminization. **Global economy.** Easing of world political tensions. Shrinking of the U.S. defense industry.

Blame the robots. Blame the women. Blame the Chinese, Japanese, Russians, Koreans, whomever or whatever you please, but recognize that the employment picture in the United States has changed forever. Between 1987 and 1992, 5.6 million people who had worked for the same employer for three or more years lost their jobs because of company failures, plant closings, job reductions, or other factors.

Manufacturing is becoming more automated and more global. The textile plants in the South and in New England don't have as many workers or managers any more, because the labels at Kmart often say, Made in China... or Taiwan... or Korea. So even though your parents could rest assured that they would have a job at the plant all their lives, you don't even know if the plant is going to be there next year.

More women are working now than ever. Statisticians call that feminization of the work force. It's a sign that the U.S. economy is shifting, or drifting, from making things to doing things. The general trends have been that men made things, or were gainfully employed in the manufacturing sector, while women did things, or were gainfully employed in the service sector. Feminization is not so much a reflection of more women working as it is a reflection of the direction of the economy.

While about two-thirds of the 5.6 million people who lost their jobs over that five-year period found work again by January 1992, about half of them were working for less money than they were before, according to a periodic survey by the U.S. Bureau of Labor Statistics. The government figures indicate that 32 percent of reemployed workers were earning 20 percent or more below their previous level of earnings, compared with 30.4 percent in 1984 and 25 percent in 1990. Only 25 percent of reemployed workers were earning 20 percent or more above their previous earnings in 1992, compared with 26 percent in 1984 and 29 percent in 1990.

Where the Jobs Are Expected to Be

If the overall economy expands at a moderate **growth** rate on average, U.S. employment is expected to reach 147.5 million people in the year 2005, including salary and wage earners and self-employed people, according to the U.S. Bureau of Labor Statistics. That would be a 22 percent growth rate from 1992 levels.

PROJECTIONS FOR GROWTH

Job Category	Growth Potential
Executive, administrative, and managerial occupations	Average
Professional specialty occupations	Faster than average
Technicians and related support occupations	Faster than average
Marketing and sales occupations	Average, but slower pace than recent years
Service occupations	Faster than average
Agriculture, forestry, fishing, and related occupations	Little or no change
Mechanics, installers, and repairers	Varies by occupation and technology advances
Construction trades and mining and drilling occupations	Average for construction; decline for extractive occupations
Production occupations	Decline, except for average growth in printing and publishing
Transportation and material moving occupations	Average
Handlers, equipment cleaners, helpers, and laborers	Average

The BLS projections are published regularly in various editions of *Occupational Outlook Quarterly*. The spring 1994 edition listed the growth prospects for various categories of occupations as the chart illustrates.

If you take recent trends and apply them to the projections, it is reasonable to assume that small businesses will account for much of the growth in jobs. The more than 6 million businesses in the United States in 1990 represented a 26 percent increase in the number of establishments since 1981. More than half, 58 percent, of the businesses had fewer than five employees. Most of these companies were retail and service businesses, and it is the service sector that is expected to experience continuing strong growth.

Chances are, you know why you want to freelance, but if you need a laundry list of possible reasons to freelance to help you stop straddling the fence, consider freelancing...

○ If you're a man in manufacturing. Men lost more jobs and regained a lesser percentage of jobs than women did during the four business cycles between 1975 and 1993. Men lost 72 percent to 100 percent of the jobs cut; women filled 51 percent to 59 percent of the jobs added. Between June 1990 and April 1993, men had a net loss of 1 million jobs, while women posted a net gain of 1.2 million jobs.

○ If you're in manufacturing, either on the assembly line or in management. The goods-producing sector suffered the heaviest losses of jobs in the recent recession. A long-term trend indicates a substantial decline in manufacturing employment in the United States, while service-producing jobs increased. Manufacturing lost more than 1.6 million jobs between 1989 and 1993.

○ If you're on the assembly line. Robots are expected to take over an increasing share of repetitive tasks performed largely by unionized workers in the past.

○ If you're in services. Even though the service sector of the economy is growing and is expected to continue to grow, more jobs are in the lower-wage category.

○ If you're a manager. The increasing shift to a global economy and the resulting competition to increase efficiency and productivity has meant the disappearance of management jobs and their lucrative salaries and benefits. Unemployment among managers shot up 55 percent during the 1991 downsizing era.

○ If you're still employed in the defense industry. Military budget cuts are expected to eliminate 1.9 million jobs by 1997.

○ If you're 55 or older. Your age group tends to require more time to find work after being displaced, an average of about 10.4 weeks, compared to 6.2 weeks for people aged 25 to 34. As discussed earlier, people enter into freelancing for a variety of reasons. Some are thrown into the job-hunting market at age 52 and, regardless of their wealth of experience, age discrimination exists.

○ If you are a woman. Government figures indicate that self-employed incorporated women earn up to 25 percent more money per hour worked than women who work for wages and salaries. Also, if you take time off for pregnancy and to spend a couple of years with your child at home, you may find that when you return to the company, you'll have to pay your dues all over again.

Rely on More Than Statistics

Rather than rely on a bunch of statistics about job growth, the lack of job growth, pay raises and how they're being doled out at smaller percentages each year, decide for yourself where to put your **trust** for the future.

You may think that with the economy improving, regular jobs are safer now than they were not so long ago, that companies are not going to be downsizing as much, and that there will continue to be growth in the number of jobs created in the nation. All of that may be true, but you have to look beneath the facade of monthly government figures and analysts' comments about them printed in the newspapers.

Look around your community, talk to your friends and neighbors, talk to your coworkers, and read the classified help-wanted ads. Compare what the national analysts are saying to the local intelligence you gather. If your freelancing is of a local nature, the national figures may not affect you at all, whether the figures are negative or positive. Even if your freelancing is regional or national, you may be in a field that is insulated at least somewhat from the macro figures.

Then, form your own view of the economic situation and how you fit into it:

O Of the jobs that are created, are they your type of job, or are they lower-paying positions?

O Have your pay raises since 1990 been greater or less each year? How about the pay raises of your coworkers and others in comparable positions at other companies?

O Does your company continue to harp on expenses and try to cut more and more corners? Has this affected the way you do your job and how you feel about what you're accomplishing at work?

You can also rely on a little animal instinct. You work long hours at the corporate office or spend a lot of time on the road for the corporate sales effort. If the dog barks at you at the back door because he no longer recognizes you, maybe it's time to install those shelves in that closet, put in that second phone line, and open a Keogh plan.

A P P E N D I X

ASSOCIATIONS AND ORGANIZATIONS

Associations and organizations are listed here for two purposes: To provide a list of organizations a freelancer can join and to provide a list of organizations that publish information a freelancer can use. For instance, a potter may want to join the American Craft Council to keep up-to-date on business news and trends related to crafting. But a management consultant or manufacturer's representative may want to survey a particular trade association's members for potential clients. Also, a number of regional or local home-based business organizations are included here.

General Associations and Organizations

American Association of Home-Based
  Businesses
P.O. Box 10023
Rockville, MD 20849
(202) 310-3130
Fax: (301) 963-7042

American Business Women's
  Association
9100 Ward Parkway · P.O. Box 8728
Kansas City, MO 64114-1728
(816) 361-6621

American Craft Council
72 Spring Street
New York, NY 10012
(212) 274-0630

American Home Business Association
4505 S. Wasatch Boulevard
Salt Lake City, UT 84124
(801) 273-5455

Association of Home-Based Businesses
136 Village Run E.
Encinitas, CA 92024
(619) 591-1151

Association of Home-Based Businesses
8348 Somerset Drive
Largo, FL 34643
(813) 539-8384

Association of Home Businesses
423 SW Fourth
Portland, OR 97204
(503) 223-1493

Brevard Home Office Association
P.O. Box 373229
Satellite Beach, FL 32937
(407) 779-9161
Fax: (407) 773-9557

Business Center for Women
571 Galapago Street
Denver, CO 80204
(303) 573-1302

Center for Family Business
5682 Mayfield Road
Cleveland, OH 44124
(216) 442-0800

Delaware Valley Home Business
  Network
(Southern New Jersey & Philadelphia
area)
P.O. Box 402
Stratford, NJ 08084
(609) 784-7268

Entrepreneurial Mothers Association
P.O. Box 2561
Mesa, AZ 85203

Entrepreneurs' Association
1609-C Ohlen Road
Austin, TX 78758
(512) 837-7737

Federation of Small Business
407 S. Dearborn, Suite 500
Chicago, IL 60605
(312) 427-0206

Freelance Editorial Association
P.O. Box 835
Cambridge, MA 02138

HBBA of Pierce and King County
2005 63d Avenue NE
Tacoma, WA 98422
(206) 927-9149

H.O.B.O. Association (Orange County)
92 Corporate Park, Suite 250
Irvine, CA 92714
(714) 261-9474

Home-Based and Small Business Special
  Interest Group (SIG) of the
  Sacramento PC Users Group
2256A Sunrise Boulevard, #607
Rancho Cordova, CA 95670
(916) 635-8044

Home-Based Business Association
919 W. Mission Drive
Chandler, AZ 85224-1958
(602) 464-0778
Fax: (602) 899-0506

Home Based Business Association of
  South Snohomish County
15248 Greenwood Avenue N.
Seattle, WA 98133
(206) 743-0779

Home Based Business Connections
P.O. Box 370646
Denver, CO 80237-0646
(303) 755-0825
Fax: (303) 337-4552

Homebased Business of Michiana
  c/o Candle Collections
61591 Bremen Highway
Mishawaka, IN 46544
(219) 259-5605

Home Based Business Owners
P.O. Box 476
South Elgin, IL 60177
(708) 888-8855

Homebased Businesswomen's
  Network, Inc.
P.O. Box 681
Newburyport, MA 01950
(508) 462-2063

The Home Business Network
4364 Bonita Road, #463
Bonita, CA 91902
(619) 479-1707

Home Business Task Force
  Associated Electric Cooperative, Inc.
2106 Jefferson Boulevard, Suite 214
Jefferson City, MO 65102
(314) 634-2454
Fax: (314) 634-3892

Home Executives National Networking
  (HENNA)
P.O. Box 6223
Bloomingdale, IL 60108-6223
(708) 307-7130
Fax: (708) 307-7140

Independent Worker's Association
448 Ignacio Boulevard, Suite 214
Navato, CA 94949
(415) 898-1580

International Association of Home-Based
Businesses
P.O. Box 4841442
Denver, CO 80248-1442
(800) 414-2422
Fax: (303) 425-9675

International Council for Small Business
3674 New York Avenue NW
Washington, DC 20005
(202) 628-8000

Mercer Island HBB Roundtable
4548 89th Avenue SE
Mercer Island, WA 98040
(206) 236-1990

Mothers' Home Business Network
P.O. Box 423
East Meadow, NY 11554
(516) 997-7394

National Association for the Cottage
Industry
P.O. Box 14460
Chicago, IL 60614
(312) 472-8116

National Association for the Self-employed
United Group Service Center
P.O. Box 1116
Hurst, TX 76053-1116
(800) 232-6273

National Association of Home-Based
Businesses
P.O. Box 30220
Baltimore, MD 21270
(410) 363-3698

National Association of Women Business
Owners
600 S. Federal Street, Suite 400
Chicago, IL 60605
(312) 922-0465

National Federation of Independent
Business, Inc.
600 Maryland Avenue SW, Suite 700
Washington, DC 20024
(202) 554-9000

National Small Business Network
P.O. Box 223
Centereach, NY 11720
(516) 467-6826

National Small Business United
1155 15th Street NW
Washington, DC 20005
(202) 293-8830

The Nebraska Development Network
Box 81
Grafton, NE 68365
(402) 282-7349

New Mexico Home Business Association
537 Franklin Street
Santa Fe, NM 87501
(508) 984-9908

North Idaho Home Business Network
1910 Meadow Lane
Post Falls, ID 83854
(208) 777-8351

Oklahoma Home-Based Business
Association
8177 S. Harvard, #107
Tulsa, OK 74137

Olympic Home-Based Business
Association
1713 E. Third Street
Port Angeles, WA 98362
(206) 452-2418
Fax: (206) 452-2418

Pittsburgh Home Business Association -
North
P.O. Box 302
Allison Park, PA 15101
(412) 486-6433

Pittsburgh Home Business Association - South
6534 Quaker Drive
Pittsburgh, PA 15236
(412) 655-7420

Sisters in Business
1107 Fair Oaks Avenue, Suite 165
South Pasadena, CA 91030
(818) 585-9353

Small Business Network
108 Hill Court

Youngsville, NC 27596
(919) 556-6808

Washington Home-Based Industry
P.O. Box 34
Shelton, WA 98584

Women's Home Business Network
2138 E. Broad Ripple Avenue, #225
Indianpolis, IN 46220
(317) 251-1131

Specialty Associations and Organizations

American Association for Medical Transcription
P.O. Box 576187
Modesto, CA 95357
(800) 982-2182

American Association of Exporters & Importers
11 W. 42d Street, 30th Floor
New York, NY 10036
(212) 944-2230

American Bakers Association
1111 14th Street NW, Suite 300
Washington, DC 20005
(202) 296-5800

American Electronics Association
5201 Great American Parkway
Santa Ana, CA 95054
(408) 987-4200

American Institute of CPAs
1211 Avenue of the Americas
New York, NY 10036
(212) 575-6200

American Society of Composers, Authors & Publishers
ASCAP Building One Lincoln Plaza
New York, NY 10023
(212) 621-6000

American Society of Interior Designers
608 Massachusetts Avenue NE
Washington, DC 20002
(202) 546-3480

American Society of Journalists and Authors, Inc.
1501 Broadway, Suite 302
New York, NY 10036
(212) 997-0947

American Society of Magazine Photographers, Inc.
419 Park Avenue S.
New York, NY 10016
(212) 889-9144

American Society of Travel Agents
1101 King Street
Alexandria, VA 22314
(703) 739-2782

American Translators Association
1735 Jefferson Davis Highway, Suite 903
Arlington, VA 22202-3413
(703) 892-1500

American Trucking Association
2200 Mill Road
Alexandria, VA 22314
(703) 838-1800

Associated Locksmiths of America
3003 Live Oak Street
Dallas, TX 75204
(214) 827-1701

Associated Master Barbers & Beauticians
of America
1318 Starbrook Drive
Charlotte, NC 28210
(704) 552-6233

Association of Independent Information
Professionals (AIIP)
c/o Burwel Enterprises, Inc.
3724 FM 1960 W., Suite 214
Houston, TX 77068
(713) 537-9051

Association of Information Imaging
Management
100 Wayne Avenue, Suite 1100
Silver Spring, MD 20910
(301) 587-8202
(Businesses in the micrographics field)

Association of Management Consultant
Firms
230 Park Avenue, Suite 544
New York, NY 10169
(212) 697-9693

Association of Shareware Professionals
545 Grover Road
Muskegon, MI 49442-9427
(616) 788-5131

Association of Venture Clubs
265 East 100 South, Suite 300
P.O. Box 3358
Salt Lake City, UT 84110-3358
(801) 364-1100

The Authors Guild, Inc.
330 W. 42d Street
New York, NY 10036-6902
(212) 563-5904

Automotive Parts & Accessories
Association
4600 East West Highway, Suite 300
Bethesda, MD 20814
(301) 459-9110

B/PAA Metroplex Corporate Center
100 Metroplex Drive
Edison, NJ 08817
(201) 985-4441
(Advertising and marketing—business to
business)

Computer Press Association
7000 Bianca Avenue
Van Nuys, CA 91411
(818) 996-7000

Direct Marketing Association
11 W. 42d Street
New York, NY 10036-8096
(212) 768-7277

Direct Selling Association
1776 K Street NW, Suite 600
Washington, DC 20006
(202) 293-5760

Electronics Industries Association
2110 Pennsylvania Avenue NW
Washington, DC 20006
(202) 457-4900

Florists Transworld Delivery Association
29200 Northwestern Highway
Southfield, MI 48034
(313) 355-9300

Graphic Artists Guild
11 W. 20th Street, 8th Floor
New York, NY 10011-3704
(212) 463-7730

Independent Computer Consultants
Association
933 Gardenview Office Parkway
St. Louis, MO 63141
(800) 438-4222 or (314) 997-4633

Independent Music Association
317 Skyline Lake Drive
P.O. Box 609
Ringwood, NJ 07456
(201) 831-1317

Information Industry Association
555 New Jersey Avenue NW, Suite 800
Washington, DC 20001
(202) 639-8262

Inland Press Association
777 Busse Highway
Park Ridge, IL 60068
(708) 696-1140
(Journalistic association for daily and
weekly publications)

International Advertising Association
342 Madison Avenue, Suite 2000
New York, NY 10173-0073
(212) 557-1133

International Association for Financial
  Planning
2 Concourse Parkway, Suite 800
Atlanta, GA 30328
(404) 395-1605 or (800) 945-IAFP

International Association of Business
  Communicators (IABC)
1 Hallidie Plaza, Suite 600
San Francisco, CA 94102
(800) 776-4222

International Car Wash Association
One East 22d Street, Suite 400
Lombard, IL 60148
(708) 495-0100

International Communications
  Industries Association
3150 Spring Street
Fairfax, VA 22031
(703) 273-7200

International Franchise Association
1350 New York Avenue NW
Washington, SC 20005
(202) 628-8000

International Reciprocal Trade
  Association
9513 Beach Mill Road
Great Falls, VA 22066
(703) 759-1473

Investigators Online Network, Ion
  Resource Line
6303 S. Rural Road, Suite #1
Temple, AZ 85283
(602) 730-8088

Manufacturers Agents Association
23016 Mill Creek Drive
Laguna Hills, CA 92653
(714) 859-4040

National Association for the Cottage
  Industry
Box 14850
Chicago, IL 60614
(312) 472-8116

National Association of Realtors
430 N. Michigan Avenue
Chicago, IL 60611
(312) 329-8200

National Association of Secretarial
  Services
3637 Fourth Street N., Suite 330
St. Petersburg, FL 33704
(813) 823-3646

National Association of Systems
  Integrators
P.O. Box 440
560 Dedham Street
Wrentham, MA 02093
(508) 384-5850

National Association of Tole and
  Decorative Artists
P.O. Box 808
Newton, KS 67114
(316) 283-9665

National Association of Wholesale
  Distributors
1725 K Street NW, Suite 710
Washington, DC 20006
(202) 872-0885

National Association of Women in
  Construction
99 Bridge Road
Hauppauge, NY 11788
(516) 348-0505

National Cosmetology Association
3510 Olive Street
St. Louis, MO 63103
(314) 534-7980

National Decorating Products
  Association
1050 N. Lindbergh Boulevard
St. Louis, MO 63132
(314) 991-3470

National Guild of Professional
  Paperhangers
136 S. Keowee Street
Dayton, OH 45402
(513) 222-9252
Fax: (513) 222 5794

National Notary Association
8236 Remmet Avenue
P.O. Box 7184
Canoga Park, CA 91304-7184
(818) 713-4000

National Pest Control Association
8100 Oak St. Dunn
Loring, VA 22027
(703) 573-8330

National Roofing Contractors
  Association
10255 W. Higgins Road, Suite 600
Rosemont, IL 60018
(708) 299-9070

National Speakers Association
3877 N. Seventh Street, Suite 350
Phoenix, AZ 85014
(602) 265-1001

National Tour Association
546 E. Main Street
Lexington, KY 40508
(606) 253-1036

Owner-Operator Independent Drivers
  Association
311 Mize Road
Grain Valley, MO 64029
(816) 229-5791

Professional Photographers of America
1090 Executive Way
Des Plaines, IL 60018
(708) 299-8161

Professional Picture Framers Association
4305 Sarellen Road
Richmond, VA 23231
(804) 226-0430

Self-Service Storage Association
60 Revere Drive, Suite 500
Northbrook, IL 60062
(708) 480-9627

Small Business Foundation of America
1155 15th Street NW
Washington, DC 20005
(202) 223-1103
(An exporting association)

Society of American Florists
1601 Duke Street
Alexandria, VA 23314
(703) 836-8700

Software Publishers Association
1730 M Street NW, Suite 700
Washington, DC 20036-4510
(202) 452-1600

Specialty Advertising Association
  International
1404 Walnut Hill Lane
Irving, TX 75038
(214) 580-0404

Trade Show Bureau
1660 Lincoln Street, Suite 2080
Denver, CO 80264
(303) 860-7626

Travel Industry Association of America
1133 21st Street NW
Washington, DC 20036
(202) 293-1433

U.S. Chamber of Commerce
1615 H Street NW
Washington, DC 20062
(202) 463-5580
(Programs and information for small

businesses; publisher of Nation's
Business magazine)

Video Retailers Association (VRA)
2455 E. Sunrise Boulevard
Ft. Lauderdale, FL 33304-1877
(305) 561-3505

Video Software Dealers Association
3 Eves Drive, Suite 307
Marlton, NJ 08053
(609) 596-8500

Women's Economic Development
Corporation
71 Vancouver Avenue, 3d Floor
New York, NY 10169
(800) 222-2933
(Business advice and workshops for
women)

Computer Services

America Online
(800) 827-6364
(703) 448-8700
fax: (800) 827-4595
Founded: 1985; members: 900,000.
Basic data: E-mail, news, sports, weather, finance, travel, shopping, and 600 bulletin-board services.
Specialities: Technical support for 300 hardware and software companies, Internet access, newspapers and magazines.

CompuServe
(800) 848-8199
(614) 457-8600
fax: (614) 457-0504
Founded: 1979; members: 1.8 million.
(The company estimates that there are

an average of six users for every one of their 300,000 accounts.)
Basic data: E-mail, news, sports, weather, reference, shopping, finance, games, travel, and 2,000 databases and discussion groups including a Working From Home Forum.
Specialities: Technical support for 700 hardware and software companies. International service that includes Germany, France, and England.

Delphi
(800) 695-4005
(617) 491-3342
Founded: 1981; members: 100,000.
Basic data: Business and finance information, real-time conferences.
Specialities: Internet, custom forums designed by members.

Dow Jones News/Retrieval
(800) 522-3567
Founded: 1974; members: 200,000.
Basic data: News, financial information, weather, and sports.
Specialities: Access to 1,500 publications, SEC and government information.

GEnie
(301) 251-6475
Founded: 1985; members: 150,000.
Basic data: E-mail, Reuters, weather, sports, travel, discussion groups, and 240 bulletin-board services.
Specialities: Internet, forums, home shopping, access to 900 newspapers and magazines, and Windows interface.

Prodigy
(800) 776-3449
Founded: 1980; members: 2 million.
Basic data: E-mail, news, sports, finance, children's education, weather, and 850 bulletin-board services.
Specialities: Prodigy news service, music, movies, interactive ESPN.

Ziff-Davis Interchange Online Network
(617) 252-5000
Founded: 1994; members: numbers not yet available.
Basic data: News, sports, weather, finance, computers.
Specialities: Group discussions, on-line reference material.

Directories

Gale Research Co., Detroit, MI, publishes a variety of directories that may be useful to freelancers, including:
Directory of Publications
Encyclopedia of Associations
Small Business Sourcebook
Trade Shows Worldwide, and
Business Organizations and Agencies Directory.

These and other directories may be available in your local or regional library.
Writer's Digest Books, Cincinnati, OH, publishes a variety of directory-type books aimed at the editorial and art occupations, including regularly updated editions of:
Writer's Market, Artist's Market, and *Photographer's Market.*

Financing Information and Financing Sources

Publications

The States and Small Business published by the SBA's Office of Advocacy is a state-by-state guide. It is available through the Government Printing Office.

Steps to Small Business Financing is a booklet developed as a joint effort by the American Bankers Association and the National Federation of Independent Business. Contact the American Bankers Association, 1120 Connecticut Avenue NW, Washington, DC 20036. Phone: (202) 663-5456.

General Information

Office of Women's Business Ownership
U.S. Small Business Administration
409 Third Street SW, 6th Floor
Washington, DC 20416
(202) 205-6673

Women's World Banking
104 E. 40th Street
New York, NY 10016
(202) 768-8513
(Has been establishing offices in other states)

Financing Sources

The National Federation of Business and Professional Women's Clubs offer members personal loans of up to $7,500 and home-equity loans up to $100,000:

National Federation of Business and
    Professional Women's Clubs, Inc.
    (BPW)
2012 Massachusetts Avenue NW
Washington, DC 20036
(800) 245-4486

Small Business Investment Companies provide venture capital to new and established small businesses:

Small Business Investment Companies
409 Third Street NW
Washington, DC 20416
(202) 205-6512

The National Association of Female Executives offers members personal credit lines up to $35,000 based on business plans and personal qualifications:

National Association of Female
Executives, Inc.
127 W. 24th Street
New York, NY 10011
(212) 645-0770

Riviera Finance has programs available to new companies and established companies with limited track records, particularly companies that may not qualify for traditional bank financing:

Riviera Finance
1171 Homestead Road, Suite 250
Santa Clara, CA 95050
(408) 248-8828

The U.S. Small Business Administration administers loan programs nationwide, and information about these programs can be obtained from local, regional, or national offices listed in various places in the government section of this appendix. The **7(a) Loan Program** constitutes more than 80 percent of all SBA business lending activity and offers three types of loans: guaranteed, direct, and immediate participation. Guaranteed loans are made by private lenders but guaranteed by the SBA. Direct loans are made to borrowers unable to obtain funds from private sources. Immediate participation loans can be funded first by either the SBA or a private lender, with the nonfunding source agreeing to participate as soon as the loan is active. The SBA can guarantee 85 percent of loans over $155,000 and 90 percent of loans under $155,000, with a maximum loan amount of $750,000. The average loan is about $175,000, extending over an eight-year period.

Decisions are based on the business owner's management ability, an effective business plan, the owner's investment, and the business's ability to repay from cash flow and profit. In general, an applicant will be required to submit the following:

o Statement of purpose for loan

o History of business

o Financial statements for the business for the past three years

o Schedule of debts

o Summary of accounts receivable and any lease arrangements

o Amount of investment owner has in business

o Projected incomes, expenses, and cash flow

o Personal financial statements

o Personal resumes

Government Agencies

The Small Business Administration (SBA) can be reached through SBA Online. The 2400-bps access numbers are (800) 859-4636 and (202) 205-7265. The 9600-bps access numbers are (800) 697-4636 and (202) 401-9600. The SBA main address is 409 Third Street SW, Washington, DC 20416. However, the agency has numerous regional offices listed in the government pages of local telephone books.

Through its Service Corps of Retired Executives (SCORE), the SBA provides a network of retired business people who volunteer their expertise through counseling or seminars.

The SBA offers an extensive selection of business-management publications, from how to start a business to exporting products. The *Small Business Directory* is a guide to this information. For a free copy write to:

SBA Publications
P.O. Box 1000
Fort Worth, TX 76119

Business Information Centers (BICs) of the U.S. Small Business Administration provide technological tools and personal counseling for prospective business owners. BICs have some of the latest in high-tech hardware, software, and telecommunications available due to sponsorship by certain manufacturers. BICs have personal computers, graphics workstations, CD-ROM technology, and interactive videos, permitting small-business starters to access market-research databases, use planning and spreadsheet software, and use vast libraries of information.

The BICs also offer one-on-one counseling with seasoned business veterans, through the Service Corps of Retired Executives (SCORE), these former executives can help prospective small-business owners develop personalized business plans.

Each BIC Offers:

o Electronic bulletin board

o Reference materials

o Computer data bases
o Texts
o On-line information exchange
o Start-up guides
o Periodicals and brochures
o Application software
o Counseling
o Computer tutorials
o Videotapes
o Interactive media
o CD-ROM libraries
o On-line research

Between the counseling and technology, BICs provide one-stop shopping for business trends and information.
BIC addresses:

Los Angeles BIC
3600 Wilshire Boulevard L-100
Los Angeles, CA 91203
(213) 251-7237

SBA - Atlanta District Office
1720 Peachtree Road NW, 6th Floor
Atlanta GA 30309
(404) 347-4749

SBA - Boston District Office
10 Causeway Street, Room 265
Boston, MA 02222-1093
(617) 565-5584

SBA - Chicago District Office
500 W. Madison Street, Suite 1250
Chicago, IL 60661-2511
(312) 353-1825

SBA - Houston District Office
9301 Southwest Freeway

Houston, TX 77074-1591
(713) 773-6595

SBA - Kansas City District Office
323 West 8th Street, Suite 501
Kansas City, MO 64105
(816) 374-6760

SBA - St. Louis District Office
815 Olive Street, Room 242
St. Louis, MO 63101
(314) 539-6600

SBA - Seattle District Office
915 Second Avenue, Suite 550
Seattle, WA 98174
(206) 220-6520

SBA - Washington District Office
1110 Vermont Avenue NW Suite 900
Washington, DC 20043-4500
(202) 606-4000 ext. 218

Other U.S. Government Resources

Publications on business management and related topics are available from the Government Printing Office (GPO). GPO bookstores are located in 24 major cities and listed in telephone directories. A Subject Bibliography is available by writing to:

Government Printing Office
Superintendent of Documents
Washington, DC 20402-9328

Other federal agencies offering publications of interest to small businesses include the U.S. Department of Agriculture and the

Environmental Protection Agency. While most publications are free, some carry a nominal fee. Regional offices of the agencies can be contacted, or you can write or call the national offices in the following list.

The Consumer Information Center offers a consumer information catalog of federal publications:

Consumer Information Center (CIC)
P.O. Box 100
Pueblo, CO 81002

The Consumer Product Safety Commission has guidelines for product safety requirements:

Consumer Product Safety Commission (CPSC)
Publications Request
Washington, DC 20207

The Department of Agriculture offers publications on selling to the USDA. Publications and programs on entrepreneurship are also available through county extension offices nationwide:

U.S. Department of Agriculture (USDA)
12th Street & Independence Avenue SW
Washington, DC 20250

The Department of Commerce's Business Assistance Center provides listings of business opportunities available in the federal government. This service also will refer businesses to different programs and services in the DOC and other federal agencies:

U.S. Department of Commerce (DOC)
Office of Business Liaison

14th Street & Constitution Avenue NW
Room 5898C
Washington, DC 20230

The Department of Labor offers publications on compliance with labor laws:

U.S. Department of Labor (DOL)
Employment Standards Administration
200 Constitution Avenue NW
Washington, DC 20210

The IRS has information and publications on tax requirements for small businesses:

U.S. Department of Treasury
Internal Revenue Service (IRS)
P.O. Box 25866
Richmond, VA 23260
(800) 424-3676

Specific publications include:

Publication 334: *Tax Guide for Small Business*
Publication 463: *Travel, Entertainment, and Gift Expenses*
Publication 541: *Tax Information on Partnerships*
Publication 542: *Tax Information on Corporations*
Publication 544: *Sales and Other Dispositions of Assets*
Publication 552: *Recordkeeping Requirements*
Publication 583: *Taxpayers Starting a Business*
Publication 587: *Business Use of Your Home*
Publication 589: *Tax Information on S Corporations*

Publication 910: *Guide to Free Tax Services*
Publication 937: *Business Reporting*

The Environmental Protection Agency offers more than 100 publications designed to help small businesses understand and comply with EPA regulations:

U.S. Environmental Protection Agency (EPA) Small Business Ombudsman
Cystal Mall - No. 2 Room 1102
1921 Jefferson Davis Highway
Arlington, VA 22202
(800) 368-5888 except in DC and VA
(703) 557-1938 in DC and VA

The Food and Drug Administration offers information on packaging and labeling requirements for food and food-related products:

U.S. Food and Drug Administration (FDA)
FDA Center for Food Safety and Applied Nutrition
200 C Street SW
Washington, DC 20204

The National Technical Information Service has a number of reports and papers available on a wide range of subjects related to small business. Many of the reports are prepared by independent consultants working under contract to the SBA's Office of Advocacy. For more information write to:

National Technical Information Service
U.S. Department of Commerce
5285 Port Royal Road
Springfield, VA 22161
(703) 487-4650

Following is a list of some of the applicable reports, their order numbers, and, if available, their prices:

How Small Businesses Learn by Sydelle Raffe, Eric Sloan, and Mary Vencill discusses the sources and value of information sought and used by small businesses. Data from a survey of 1,247 businesses between February 22 and March 30, 1994, are available on diskette. Full report cost: $27. Order number: PB95-100293.

Environmental Financial Responsibility by Robert E. Burt discusses federal environmental mandates, their impact on small businesses, and sources of funding available to comply with regulations. Cost: $19.50. Order number: PB95-100301.

Programs to Improve Health Insurance Access for Small Business: What Works and What Doesn't by Zachary Dyckman, Ph.D., and Joanna Burnette analyzes the state of health insurance in small business. It identifies and reviews 27 programs that have been successful or show promise of success in expanding health-insurance coverage for small firms. Order number: PB92-183607.

Measuring the Uninsured by Firm Size and Employment Status: Variation in Health Insurance Coverage Rates (Part I) by Mark C. Berger, Dan A. Black, and Frank A. Scott focuses on the extent of insured and uninsured individuals within the context of business size and employment status. Among the findings:

o Workers in small firms are significantly more likely to be uninsured than workers in large firms. In 1992, 25.9 percent of private, nonagricultural wage-and-salary workers in firms with fewer than 25 employees lacked some form of health insurance, compared with 10.3 percent of workers in firms with 500 or more employees.

o The unincorporated self-employed are less likely to have health insurance than are the incorporated self-employed. In 1992, 23.9 percent of the unincorporated self-employed lacked health insurance coverage from any source, compared with 9.1 percent of the incorporated self-employed.

Order number: PB94-195153.

Myths and Realities of Working at Home: Characteristics of Homebased Business Owners and Telecommuters by Joanne H. Pratt discusses characteristics of home-based workers compared to people who work outside the home. Data from the Bureau of Labor Statistics' National Longitudinal Survey were used for the research. Among the findings:

o There is little difference in the profile characteristics of business owners who work at home and those who do not.

o Home-based businesses have greater net worth than non-home-based businesses.

o Telecommuters have positive attitudes toward their work. They like the kind of work they do, they do not feel isolated from their peers, and they enjoy considerable job stability.

Order number: PB93-192862.

Miscellaneous Sources of Help

Many colleges and universities have programs specially designed to help small businesses get up and running. Some of these programs even have home-based components. It's worth a call to your local college to find out.

Also, many local school systems offer numerous continuing education courses that freelancers can use, such as accounting, desktop publishing, photography, and woodworking. The courses are generally inexpensive and taught one or two nights a week for several weeks.

The SBA also administers the Small Business Development Center Program, with cooperative funding and effort provided by local and state governments, educational institutions, and private enterprise. A network of almost 60 Small Business Development Centers exists, covering all 50 states, the District of Columbia, Puerto Rico, and the Virgin Islands. Extending from those SBDCs are more than 700 locations at which a prospective or current business owner can obtain information and counseling. Subcenters are located at colleges, universities, community colleges, vocational schools, chambers of commerce, and economic development corporations.

The purpose of SBDCs is to provide up-to-date counseling, training, and technical assistance in business management. They also aid in applying for Small Business Innovation and Research grants from the federal government. These services are available to people starting or operating a small business who cannot afford private consultants.

Business and Freelancing Terms

account In freelancing, an "account" is sometimes synonymous with "client." In bookkeeping, an account is the record-keeping entry for a customer, client, or supplier. An *account payable* is an amount owed to someone. An *account receivable* is an amount someone owes you.

account executive In advertising, one who supervises an account.

accrual basis accounting Method of accounting in which income is reported when earned, but not necessarily collected, and expenses are reported when incurred, not necessarily paid. This method allows a more total and clearer picture of income and expense relationships than **cash basis accounting**.

asset Money or property owned by a business or individual. See **liability**.

break even When a business neither loses money nor makes a profit.

camera-ready art In publishing or advertising, the stage at which a piece is ready to be photographed by processing cameras for final printing. Ad fees are based on an adver-tiser supplying camera-ready art. Often, an additional fee is charged if an ad also has to be designed and produced.

capital Money or material on hand or being used by a business.

cash basis accounting Method of accounting in which sales are recorded when cash is received and expenses are recorded when cash is disbursed. Basically, a checkbook register is a cash-basis system of accounting. See **accrual basis accounting**.

cash flow Money comes in. Money goes out. The balance between the two directions represents the flow.

certified public accountant An accountant becomes a *CPA* by passing a rigorous, uniform test developed by the Institute of Certified Public Accountants.

circulation In advertising, fees can be partially determined based on the number of copies a publication sells through subscription and newsstand and whether copies are purchased, sent free, or mailed as a portion of membership benefits. Typically, the higher the circulation, the higher the advertising fee. See **column** and **readership.**

collateral Property or other asset that is pledged against a debt obligation. Often, the collateral is the property for which the money was borrowed.

column In advertising and publishing, the basic unit of text in a newspaper, magazine, book, or other publication. A column is typically measured by **pica** width and by inch depth, such as 23 picas wide, 7 inches deep. When purchasing advertising, you often specify ad size in terms of columns; for instance, you might buy a 2-column-by-4-inch ad in a magazine. The ad's size and the magazine's **circulation** are two factors used to determine the cost of the advertising.

demographics Statistical characteristics of a population. This includes information such as age, gender, income, ethnicity, marital status, and home ownership percentage. A freelancer may, for instance, want to know the demographics of a particular section of his or her state.

desktop publishing Design and composition of published materials using commonly available computer equipment and specialized software.

draw Cash a sole proprietor or partner takes out of the business for personal use during an accounting period. It

is similar to gross income on a payroll check, i.e., income before taxes.

electronic files Specific entities stored on your computer's hard disk or on other disks, such as floppies or compact discs.

equity The value of assets, excluding any related liabilities. If you own a home worth $100,000, and you owe the bank $65,000, your equity equals $35,000, or 35 percent of your home's value.

four-color process The method printers use to produce full-color materials. All printed colors are composed of varying percentages of four basic colors: cyan (blue), magenta (red), yellow, and black.

hardware In computers, the physical equipment you see and use. See **software.**

joint venture A specific legal or management arrangement in which two or more parties agree to participate in a project. Unlike a partnership, a joint venture typically has a defined scope and time frame.

layout and design How a published piece, such as an ad or magazine, is arranged graphically.

ledger The "book" in which you record income and expenses. It can be a physical book with paper pages or an electronic one composed of computer files.

liability An obligation or debt.

loss A negative figure that results when expenses and deductions are greater than income.

modem Computer hardware that enables your computer to use telephone lines to connect to other computers. A fax/modem enables you to also send and receive faxes electronically. Modems require specially designed software, which often is bundled with the modem or with the computer system.

news release/press release A letter-form announcement of a newsworthy event, product, or service. It usually starts with the specified date on which the information in the release is available for use, then it proceeds to explain the *who, what, when, where, how,* and *why* of the release. It may be one element of a **press kit.**

on-line service A company that provides the means by which you can send and receive various items via computer modem.

operating statement An accounting sheet showing all income, expenses, and the net **profit** or **loss** of a business during a specified period of time.

pica A standard measurement used in printing. Six picas are approximately equivalent to one inch.

presentation A demonstration performed to accomplish a certain goal.

A freelancer would make a presentation, typically including verbal and visual elements, to show a client that the freelancer is worthy of being hired for a certain job.

presentation software Computer software that enables one to design visual elements to be used in a presentation, including 35mm slides with dramatic charts and graphs. The computer files are electronically sent via modem to a service company, which turns the electronic information into physical slides; the slides are then returned by mail or courier within a few days.

press kit A planned package of promotional and news items about a company, product, or individual. Elements can include a **news release,** a brochure, a photograph, a fact sheet, and a business card. Kits are often enclosed in a specially designed folder.

profit A gain in money or property after all expenses and deductions have been deducted. See **loss.**

programming In computers, the process of writing or editing software so that it performs certain tasks in specified ways.

readership In publishing, the estimated number of people who read a publication. Since a newspaper is delivered to a household, where usually more than one person reads it, newspaper publishers multiply their

circulation figures by certain factors to arrive at their readership.

software In computers, the programs that tell the **hardware** what to do and how to do it. See **programming.**

spreadsheet On paper, a columnar layout in which rows of numbers are entered to make certain calculations, such as determining the amount spent on one item during each month of the year. In computers, a spreadsheet program automates many of the functions, making it easier to manipulate numbers to test different scenarios, such as studying the effects of various cost cuts on the projected year-end profit.

word-processing program Computer software used to perform a range of tasks, from writing notes and letters to making up a simple newsletter.

worker's compensation To an employer, the amount paid to cover an employee's injury on the job. Worker's compensation insurance is required by law for companies with one or more employees.

For Further Reading

Books
Advertising and Marketing

Brabec, Barbara. *Crafts Marketing Success Secrets*. Naperville, IL: Barbara Brabec Productions, 1991.

Brodsky, Bart, and Janet Geis. *Finding Your Niche—Marketing Your Professional Service*. Community Resource Institute Press, 1992.

Burgett, Gordon. *Niche Marketing for Writers, Speakers, and Entrepreneurs—How to Make Yourself Indispensable, Slightly Immortal, and Lifelong Rich in 18 Months*. Northglenn, CO: Communication Unlimited, 1993.

Davidson, Jeffrey P. *Marketing Your Home-Based Business*. Bob Adams, 1990.

Fletcher, Tana, and Julia Rockler. *Getting Publicity—A Do-It-Yourself Guide for Small Business and Non-Profit Groups*. Bellingham, WA: Self-Counsel Press, 1990.

McIntyre, Catherine V. *Writing Effective News Releases—How to Get Free Publicity for Yourself, Your Business, or Your Organization*. Piccadilly Books, 1992.

Lant, Jeffrey. *Cash Copy—How to Offer Your Products and Services So Your Prospects Buy Them...Now*. Cambridge, MA: Jeffrey Lant Associates, 1992.

Phillips, Michael, and Salli Rasberry. *Marketing Without Advertising—Creative Strategies for Small Business Success*. Berkeley, CA: Nolo Press, 1989.

Ross, Marilyn, and Tom Ross. *Big Ideas for Small Service Businesses—How to Successfully Advertise, Publicize, and Maximize Your Business or Professional Practice*. Buena Vista, CO: Communication Creativity, 1993.

Swanson, Doug. *Business Building...in the '90s—A Complete Guide to Promoting and Marketing Your*

Service Business. Lawton, OK: The Swanson Group, 1992.

Waldrop, Judith, with Marcia Mogelonsky. *The Seasons of Business. The Marketer's Guide to Consumer Behavior.* Ithaca, NY: American Demographics Books, 1992.

Finance

Bangs, David H., Jr. *The Cash Flow Control Guide—Methods to Understand and Control the Small Business's Number One Problem.* Dover, NH: Upstart Publishing, 1990.

Fleury, Robert E. *The Small Business Guide: How to Manage Your Cash, Profits and Taxes.* Naperville, IL: Sourcebooks Trade, 1992.

McQuown, Judith H. *Inc. Yourself: How to Profit by Setting Up Your Own Corporation.* New York: Harper-Collins, 1992.

Ray, Norm. *Easy Financials for Your Home-Based Business: The Friendly Guide to Successful Management Systems for Busy Home Entrepreneurs.* Windsor, CA: Rayve Productions, Inc., 1992.

General Business

Alarid, William, and Gustav Berle. *Free Help From Uncle Sam to Start Your Own Business (Or Expand the One You Have).* Santa Monica, CA: Puma Publishing, 1992.

Anthony, Joseph. *Kiplinger's Working for Yourself: Full Time, Part Time, Anytime.* Washington: Kiplinger Books, 1993.

Arden, Lynie. *101 Franchises You Can Run From Home.* New York: John Wiley & Sons, 1990.

Attard, Janet. *The Home Office and Small Business Answer Book.* New York: Henry Holt, 1993.

Baber, Anne, and Lynne Waymon. *Great Connections—Small Talk and Networking for Businesspeople.* Waymon & Associates, 1992.

Brabec, Barbara. *Homemade Money.* 5th ed. Cincinnati, OH: Betterway Books, 1994.

Cook, Mel. *Home Business—Big Business: How to Launch Your Home Business and Make It a Success.* New York: Collier Books, 1992.

Cross, Wilbur. *Growing Your Small Business Made Simple.* New York: Doubleday, 1993.

Davidson, Robert L. *Contracting Your Services.* New York: John Wiley & Sons, 1990.

Day, John. *Small Business in Tough Times.* San Diego: Pfeiffer & Co., 1993.

Edwards, Sarah, and Paul Edwards. *The Best Home Businesses for the 90s.*

Los Angeles: Jeremy P. Tarcher, Inc., 1991.

Edwards, Sarah, and Paul Edwards. *Making It On Your Own*. Los Angeles: Jeremy P. Tarcher, Inc., 1991.

Edwards, Sarah, and Paul Edwards. *Working From Home*. Los Angeles: Jeremy P. Tarcher, Inc./Perigee, 1990.

Eyler, David R. *The Executive Moonlighter: Building Your Next Career Without Leaving Your Present Job*. New York: John Wiley & Sons, 1989.

Fields, Louis W., and Richard R. Gallagher. *Bookkeeping Made Simple*. New York: Doubleday, 1990.

Frohbieter-Mueller, Jo. *Your Home Business Can Make Dollars and Sense*. Radnor, PA: Chilton Book Co., 1990.

Gallagher, Richard R. *Your Small Business Made Simple*. New York: Doubleday, 1989.

Hahn, Harley, and Rick Stout. *The Internet Yellow Pages*. Berkeley, CA: Osborne McGraw-Hill, 1994.

Hall, Daryl Allen. *1001 Jobs You Can Start From Home*. New York: John Wiley & Sons, 1992.

Hausman, Carl. *Moonlighting. 148 Great Ways to Make Money on the Side*. New York: Avon Books, 1989.

Holland, Philip, *How to Start a Business Without Quitting Your Job: The Moonlight Entrepreneur's Guide*. Berkeley, CA: Ten Speed Press, 1992.

Holtz, Herman. *The Complete Work-At-Home Companion*. Rocklin, CA: Prima Publishing, 1990.

Kamoroff, Bernard. *Small Time Operator—How to Start Your Own Business, Keep Your Books, Pay Your Taxes, and Stay Out of Trouble*. Laytonville, CA: Bell Springs Publishing. Revised annually.

Kishel, Gregory, and Patricia Kishel. *Start, Run, and Profit from Your Own Home-Based Business*. New York: John Wiley & Sons, Inc., 1991.

Lasher, William. *The Perfect Business Plan Made Simple*. New York: Doubleday, 1994.

Luther, William. *The Start-Up Business Plan*. New York: Prentice Hall, 1991.

Matusky, Gregory. *The Best Home-Based Franchises*. New York: Doubleday, 1992.

Parson, Mary Jean. *Financially Managing the One-Person Business*. Los Angeles: Perigee, 1991.

PSI Successful Business Library. *Starting and Operating a Business* Series. Grants Pass, OR: The Oasis Press/PSI Research.

Radin, Bill. *Breakaway Careers.* Hawthorne, NJ: Career Press, 1994.

Revel, Chase. *184 Businesses Anyone Can Start and Make a Lot of Money.* New York: Bantam Books, 1991.

Revel, Chase. *168 More Businesses Anyone Can Start and Make a Lot of Money.* New York: Bantam Books, 1991.

Ross, Marilyn, and Tom Ross. *Country Bound! How to Trade Business Suit Blues for Blue Jean Dreams.* Buena Vista, CO: Communication Creativity, 1992.

Shingleton, John D., and James Anderson. *Mid-Career Changes: Strategies for Success.* Career Publishing, 1993.

Waxler, Myer, and Robert W. Wolf. *Good-Bye Job, Hello Me: Self-Discovery Through Self-Employment.* New York: Scott, Foresman, 1987.

Whittlesey, Marietta. *The New Freelancer's Handbook: Successful Self-Employment.* New York: Simon & Schuster, 1988.

Home-Office Management

Alvarez, Mark. *Home Office Book: How to Set Up an Efficient Personal Workspace in the Computer Age.* Woodbury, CT: Goodwood Press, 1990.

Atkinson, William. *Working at Home: Is It for You?* New York: Dow Jones-Irwin, 1985.

Beach, Betty. *Integrating Work and Family Life: The Home-Working Family.* New York: State University of New York Press, 1989.

Hemphill, Barbara. *Taming the Paper Tiger: Organizing the Paper in Your Life.* Washington: Kiplinger Books, 1992.

Kanarek, Lisa. *Organizing Your Home Office for Success—Expert Strategies That Can Work for You.* New York: NAL/Dutton (Plume), 1993.

Katz, Patricia. *Getting It Together—How to Organize Your Work, Your Home and Yourself.* Canada: Centrax Books, 1992.

Martin, Diana, and Mary Cropper. *Fresh Ideas in Letterheads & Business Card Design.* Cincinnati: North Light Books, 1993.

Parson, Mary Jean. *Managing the One-Person Business.* New York: Putnum, 1990.

Schreiber, Norman. *Your Home Office.* New York: Harper & Row, 1990.

Stern, Linda. *Bookkeeping on Your Home-Based PC.* New York: Windcrest/McGraw-Hill, 1993.

Sullivan, Nick. *Computer Power for Your Small Business.* New York: AMACOM, 1990.

Yager, Jan. *Making Your Office Work for You—How to Create a Sense of Comfort, Efficiency & Ease in Your Work Space.* New York: Doubleday, 1989.

Law

Diamond, Michael R., and Julie L. Williams. *How to Incorporate. A Handbook for Entrepreneurs and Professionals.* Second Edition. New York: John Wiley & Sons, 1993.

Fishman, Anthony Stephen. *The Copyright Handbook—How to Protect and Use Written Works.* Berkeley, CA: Nolo Press, 1992.

Sanderson, Steve. *Standard Legal Forms and Agreements for Small Business.* Bellingham, WA: Self-Counsel Press, 1990.

Sitarz, Daniel. *The Desktop Publisher's Legal Handbook: A Comprehensive Guide to Computer Publishing Law.* Carbondale, IL: Nova Publishing Co., 1989.

Sitarz, Daniel. *The Complete Book of Small Business Legal Forms.* Carbondale, IL: Nova Publishing Co., 1991.

Specific Occupations

Anderson, Scott. *Desktop Publishing: Dollars and Sense.* Hillsboro, OR: Blue Heron Publishers, 1992.

Aslett, Don, and Mark Browning. *Cleaning Up for a Living.* Crozet, VA: Betterway Books, 1991.

Benzel, Rick. *Health Service Businesses on Your Home-Based PC.* New York: Windcrest, 1993.

Biehl, Stewart P. *How to Succeed as an Artist in Your Home Town.* Cincinnati: North Light Books, 1992.

Blanchard, Marjorie P. *Cater From Your Own Kitchen.* New York: Bobbs-Merrill Co., 1981.

Bond, William J. *Home-Based Catalog Marketing: A Success Guide for Entrepreneurs.* New York: McGraw-Hill, 1994.

Bond, William J. *Home-Based Newsletter Publishing: A Success Guide for Entrepreneurs.* New York: McGraw-Hill, 1992.

Brabec, Barbara. *Creative Cash—How to Sell Your Crafts, Needlework, Designs and Know-How.* Naperville, IL: Barbara Brabec Productions, 1993.

Brodsky, Bart, and Janet Geis. *The Teaching Marketplace—Make Money With Freelance Teaching, Corporate Trainings, and on the Lecture Circuit.* Community Resource Institute Press, 1991.

Cohen, William. *Building a Mail Order Business: A Complete Manual for Success.* New York: John Wiley & Sons, 1991.

Collier, David, and Bob Cotton. *Basic Desktop Design & Layout.* Cincinnati: North Light Books, 1989.

Cribb, Larry. *How You Can Make $25,000 a Year With Your Camera No Matter Where You Live*. Cincinnati: Writer's Digest Books, 1991.

Dearing, James. *Making Money Making Music (No Matter Where You Live)*. Cincinnati: Writer's Digest, 1990.

Fleishman, Michael. *Getting Started as a Freelance Illustrator or Designer*. Cincinnati, OH: North Light Books, 1990.

Gallagher, Patricia C. *Start Your Own At-Home Child Care Business*. New York: Doubleday, 1989.

Glenn, Peggy. *Making Money Typing at Home—Everything You Need to Start, Run and Succeed in Your Own Typing Business at Home*. Huntington Beach, CA: Aames-Allen, 1990.

Glenn, Peggy. *Word Processing Profits at Home: A Complete Business Plan*. Huntington Beach, CA: Aames-Allen, 1992.

Gordon, Elliott, and Barbara Gordon. *How to Sell Your Photographs and Illustrations*. Cincinnati: North Light Books, 1990.

Green, Mary. *How to Be an Importer and Pay for Your World Travel*. Berkeley, CA: Ten Speed Press, 1993.

Harris, Catherine. *Cash From Your Kitchen*. New York: Holt, Rinehart and Winston, 1984.

Hartonczyk, Chef William, and Christina Hartonczyk. *Catering for Profit—How to Make Money on Your Favorite Recipes*. Scottsdale, AZ: Progeny Publishing, 1993.

Heron, Michal. *How to Shoot Stock Photos That Sell*. Cincinnati: Writer's Digest Books, 1990.

Hodson, Marcia. *Word Processing Plus—Profiles of Home-Based Success*. Galveston, IN: CountrySide Publications, 1991.

Holtz, Herman. *How to Start and Run a Writing & Editing Business*. New York: John Wiley & Sons, 1992.

Jacobs, Lou. *Selling Stock Photography: How to Market Your Photographs for Maximum Profit*. New York: Amphoto, 1992.

Jorwik, F.X. *The Greenhouse and Nursery Handbook—A Complete Guide to Growing and Selling Ornamental Plants*. Andmar Press, 1992.

Lawrence, Elizabeth. *The Complete Caterer: A Practical Guide to the Craft and Business of Catering*. New York: Doubleday, 1992.

Levoy, Gregg. *This Business of Writing*. Cincinnati: Writer's Digest Books, 1992.

Long, Steve, and Cindy Long. *"You Can Make Money From Your Arts and Crafts."* Scotts Valley, CA: Mark Publishing, 1988.

Neff, Jack. *Make Your Woodworking Pay for Itself.* Cincinnati: Writer's Digest Books, 1992.

Oberrecht, Kenn. *How to Open and Operate a Home-Based Photography Business.* Old Saybrook, CT: Globe Pequot Press, 1993.

Parker, Roger C. *Newsletters From the Desktop: Designing Effective Publications With Your Computer.* Chapel Hill, NC: Ventana Press, 1990.

Schiffman, Stephan. *The Consultant's Handbook: How to Start & Develop Your Own Practice.* Boston: Bob Adams Inc., 1988.

Silliphant, Leigh, and Sureleigh. *Making $70,000-Plus a Year as a Self-Employed Manufacturer's Representative.* Berkeley, CA: Ten Speed Press, 1988.

Smith, Brian R. *How to Become Successfully Self-Employed.* Boston: Bob Adams Inc., 1991.

Stankus, Jan. *How to Open and Operate a Bed & Breakfast Home.* Chester, CT: Globe Pequot Press, 1992.

Stewart, Joyce. *How to Make Your Design Business Profitable.* Cincinnati: North Light Books, 1992.

Sturdivant, Lee. *Flowers for Sale: Growing and Marketing Cut Flowers—Backyard to Small Acreage; A Bootstrap Guide.* Friday Harbor, WA: San Juan Naturals, 1992.

Sykes, Barbara Wright. *The "Business" of Sewing.* Chino Hills, CA: Collins Publications.

Wilbur, L. Perry. *Money in Your Mailbox: How to Start and Operate a Mail-Order Business.* New York: John Wiley & Sons, 1992.

Zuckerman, Jim. *The Professional Photographer's Guide to Shooting and Selling Nature and Wildlife Photos.* Cincinnati: Writer's Digest Books, 1991.

Catalogs of Publishers Specializing in Small and Home-Based Business

The Entrepreneur's Business Success Resource Guide. Aegis Publishing Group, 796 Aquidneck Ave., Newport, RI 02840.

Self Counsel Press Catalog. Self-Counsel Press, 1704 N. State Street, Bellingham, WA 98225.

TAB Books Catalog. TAB Books, Inc., Blue Ridge Summit, PA 17294.

Upstart Catalog. Upstart Publishing Company, Inc., 12 Portland St., Dover, NH 03820.

The Whole Work Catalog. New Careers Center, P.O. Box 2193, Boulder, CO 80306.

The Writer's Digest and *North Light Books Catalog*. Writer's Digest/ North Light Books, 1507 Dana Ave., Cincinnati, OH 45207.

Magazines and Other Periodicals

Many magazines and periodicals that relate to home-based occupations are readily available on newsstands. These include a plethora of computer magazines, but one that focuses on freelancing issues is *Home Office Computing*. If you're looking for business start-up ideas, try something like Income Opportunities. Some publications are geared toward specific occupations, such as *Advertising Age*, *Writer's Digest*, and *Woodshop News*.

A number of trade publications exist, available through subscription only or as a benefit of belonging to a trade association or business organization. Some trade magazines require you to "qualify" as a subscriber by specifying your degree of participation in a particular business category, such as sales, management, technical, or consultant.

To see a list of publications and determine which ones you may want to review, check your local library's reference section for a guide to periodicals.

There are also a number of periodicals aimed specifically at home-based businesses, including the *National Home Business Report — The Voice of America's Oldest Home-Business Network* (Barbara Brabec, publisher, P.O. Box 2137, Naperville, IL 60567) and *Home Office Opportunities* (P.O. Box 780, Lyman, WY 82937).

Published Articles

"Going I-Way?" Series of articles about conducting business on the Internet. *PC Computing*. September 1994.

"The Intelligent Home Office." *Working Woman Magazine*. December 1993.

Online Access, October 1994 issue has two articles on starting and running a computer bulletin board. "So You Want to Be a Ssysop," by George V. Hulme, and "Selecting Your BBS Software," by Jack M. Germain. The issue also contains a BBS Phone Book.

"Out on a limb: bold prediction # 5." *Inc.* May 1993.

"Working for yourself." *The Economist*. August 29, 1992.

Anthony, Joseph. "Maybe you should buy a business." *Kiplinger's Personal Finance Magazine*. May 1993.

Black, Pam. "A home office that's easier on the eyes—and the back." *Business Week*. August 17, 1992.

Bott, Catherine A. "Home is where the office is." *Real Estate Today*. March 1993.

Brennan, William. "Home sweet home: important tax facts for home offices, computers and cellular phones." *Financial World*. February 15, 1994.

Buskin, John. "Isolation paranoia." *Home Office Computing*. January 1994.

Case, John. "How to survive without a job." *Inc.* June 1992.

Casey, Patricia. "How not to irk the IRS: avoiding these six red flags can keep you off the audit hit list." *Black Enterprise*. January 1994.

Chien, Philip. "The frontiers of space." *Compute*. September 1992.

Clark, Gerald. "Cottage Industry." *Reader's Digest*. October 1992.

Crosby, Bill. "Squeezing a home office into an attic." *Sunset*. April 1993.

Davis, Kristin. "Financial planning for erratic incomes." *Kiplinger's Personal Finance Magazine*. April 1992.

Dunkin, Amy. "Don't leave your home office uncovered." *Business Week*. March 25, 1991.

Dvorak, John C. "SOHO? Ho ho!" *PC Magazine*. January 25, 1994.

Edwards, Paul, and Sarah. "Making the small office work." *Newsweek*. November 22, 1993.

Follis, John. "Free advice: tips for the hopeful independent creative, now that unemployment is the order of the day and freelancing is more than just another word for nothing left to lose." *Advertising Age*. January 13, 1992.

Gabriel, Gail. "Please, do not disturb!" *Home Office Computing*. January 1994.

Gelband, Joseph F. "Nice commute but writeoffs for home offices are tricky." *Barron's*. December 27, 1993.

Gunnerson, Ronnie. "Agent on a mission." *Home Office Computing*. June 1991.

Gunnerson, Ronnie. "Success on her own terms." *Home Office Computing*. June 1991.

Harris, Patricia, and David Lyon. "Home Work." Plus other related articles. *CompuServe Magazine*. August 1994.

Henderson, Nancy. "Weeding out your home files." *Changing Times*. January 1991.

Henderson, Nancy. "Cutting insurance costs when you're self-employed." *Kiplinger's Personal Finance Magazine*. April 1992.

Herman, Tom. "Home-office deductions are possible." *The Wall Street Journal*. March 25, 1994.

Hotch, Ripley. "All the comforts of a home office." *Nation's Business*. July 1993.

Jones, Ted, and Pat McMillan. "Creative home offices: built-ins to help you merge professional and private lives." *Home Mechanix*. March 1991.

Krunemaker, Larry. "Searching for affordable health insurance." *Home Office Computing*. March 1993.

Mandel, Michael J. "When the going gets tough, the tough get self-employed." *Business Week*. July 22, 1991.

Mahar, Maggie. "White-collar wash: for women, more jobs, less $. *Working Women*. March 1994.

Matthews, Richard. "How to start a country business." *Country Journal*. July/August, 1992.

McCarroll, Thomas. "Starting over." *Time*. January 6, 1992.

Murphy, Anne, and Phaedra Hise. "Do-It-Yourself Job Creation." *Inc*. January 1994.

O'Malley, Christopher. "The well-connected office." *Popular Science*. October 1992.

Peterson, Dart G., Jr. "On lessons learned and relearned." *Technical Communication*. February 1991.

Razzi, Elizabeth. "Keeping your home business neighborly." *Kiplinger's Personal Finance Magazine*. November 1993.

Robotham, Tom. "How to have a great job...without leaving home." *Cosmopolitan*. February 1994.

Roha, Ronaleen R. "A winning game plan: small businesses can flourish even in times like these." *Changing Times*. February 1991.

Roha, Ronaleen R. "Call your own shots." *Kiplinger's Personal Finance Magazine*. June 1992.

Ryans, Cynthia C. "Self-employed in your own business." *Journal of Small Business Management*. July 1991.

Ryans, Cynthia C. "Self-employment retirement plans. *Journal of Small Business Management*. July 1991.

Ryans, Cynthia C. "Self-employment tax." *Journal of Small Business Management*. July 1991.

Schreiber, Norman, and Christopher Meeks. "Home is where the office is." *Writer's Digest*. December 1991.

Silvestri, George T. "Who are the self-employed?" *Occupational Outlook Quarterly*. Spring 1991.

Statin, Peter D. "IRS seeks to alter hiring practices." *Architectural Record*. April 1992.

Stern, Linda. "Can you quit your day job?" *Home Office Computing*. March 1993.

Stone, Amey. "Insuring home and office when home is the office." *Business Week*. November 1, 1993.

Solomon, Barbara. "Get your benefits." *Writer's Digest*. January 1994.

Sullivan, Nick. "The ultimate home office: the White House." *Home Office Computing*. February 1992.

Szabo, Joan C. "How to survive an IRS audit. *Nation's Business*. April 1994.

Toussaint, Pamela. "Plugged in for business." *Black Enterprise*. October 1991.

Whalen, Jean. "Free-lancer hot line aids minorities." *Advertising Age*. September 27, 1993.

Williams, Gurney III. "The self-employment urge." *The American Legion*. January 1992.

Index

A

accounting advice, seeking   94, 138
advertising and public relations agent
25-26
advertising
    consultant   38
    types of   123-124
answering device, telephone   84
association addresses   159-167
attitude, professional   81

B

baker   110
balance, business and personal lives   72
barter   82-84
blacksmithing   28
bookkeeper   26-27
bookkeeping   114-115
budget   56, 111, 141
business license   93
business plan   139
buying in bulk   143

C

cakes, specialty   140
caterer/catering   60, 98
cash flow   19-20, 115-117, 141-142
communicating   125-126

commuting   16
competency   25
competition, analyzing   57-59
computer bulletin board system   24
computer consultant   27, 38, 58, 82
computer services, on-line   51, 166-167
computer system, how to buy   84-88
computers, working with   24
contacts   49-50
contract
    elements of   102
    standard   93, 102
corporation   96-97, 134
costs, direct and indirect   107
coworkers   76
craft artisan   27-28, 60
craft shows   60, 120

D

debt, personal   114
desktop publishing   28-29, 58
directories   167
discipline   41

E

editorial services   33-34
elderly assistance service   29-30
electronic mail, or e-mail   50-51

employment projections   153–154
entrepreneur, compared to freelancer 23
expansion, of existing business   133–135
expenses, controlling   113
experience   38–40

F
family considerations   21, 71–72, 76–79
fax machine   84
fencing business   122
fictitious name   93, 100
financing
   information and sources   167–169
   options   111, 132
finances, separating personal and business 105
flexibility   17
focus, on goals, etc.   73
follow-up   122
freelancer/freelancing
   A–Z   42
   by gender   48–49
   compared to entrepreneur   23
   business vs. dream   56
   qualities of   38
   types of   11–12
furniture, office   82
furniture restorer/refinisher   30–31, 38
furniture refinisher   82

G
goals, personal and professional   73–75
government agencies   169–173

H
hobby   128
hobby to profession   128–131
home-based business, defined   46
home-based worker, defined   46
home-grown ingenuity   119
home-office deduction   112

honesty   41–43

I
image, professional   81, 126, 133
independent contractor   100–102
insurance
   automobile   103
   disability   102, 145
   health   57, 103, 105, 144–145
   homeowner's   146
   life   146
   liability   93, 102
Internet   51–52
inventory   82
isolation   45, 49

J
juggler   37, 40

K
Keough Plan   147–148

L
legal advice, seeking   94, 138
librarian   130
listening, importance of   148–149

M
marketing a service   120–122
marketing plan   119–120
mistakes, common   138
money management   132
moonlighting   131

N
networking   49

O
office layout, sample   83
office politics   19
on-line computer services   51–52, 166–167
organization chart, one-person   50

overhead 107

P

pajamas test 39
partnership 95–96
part-time to full-time freelancing 59, 131
pet-sitting service 60, 124
philosophical questions 74
photographer 82
photographer's lab 81
planning 17, 21, 62–65
potter 27, 82
pricing 105–111, 132
printers, computer 87
priorities 17, 65
profit 105–111
profit-and-loss statement 148
project plan 62–65
promotional products 124–125
public relations 113, 124–125
public relations agent 25

Q

quick turnaround, scheduling for 67

R

record keeping 114–115, 149
resource, assigning to tasks 64
retirement planning 146–147

S

sales representative 134
schedule 61, 67
Schedule C 46–47
scope
   of business 139–140
   of work 62–64
seasonal considerations 59

self-confidence 40
self-employed 46
self-employment tax 103
self-reliance 18, 40
self-sufficiency 16
seminars 60
service, marketing of 120–122
software, computer 88
   and record keeping 114–117
sole proprietorship 95, 134
subcontracting 134

T

task list 62–64
tax identification number 94, 100
taxes
   sales 94
   savings tips 142
teachers 130
time, billable 107–109
time management 66–67
tools, professional vs. amateur 82
tools of the trade 82

V

videographer 31

W

will 93, 102
wish list 82
woodworker 25, 32, 40, 82, 120
woodworker's bench 81
work habits 19
writer 82
writing and editorial services 33–34

Z

zoning 93, 98–100

ABOUT THE AUTHOR

Larry E. Hand has worked as a freelancer to some degree—moonlighting to full-time—for 20 years. Most recently, he was co-editor (with his wife Margaret Heinrich Hand, also a freelancer) of the 1994 and 1995 editions of the *Science Yearbook* for the *Young Students Learning Library*® (Newfield Publications). As a writer, photographer, and editor, he has worked for major daily newspapers, national magazines, corporate communications offices, and government agencies. He is managing editor of a reference-book revision project in which the final product (scheduled for 1996 publication) will be a 6-million-word, 2,500-page work, much of it based on research and writing done by freelancers.